EDUCATION IN A COMPETITIVE AND GLOBALIZING WORLD

IMPROVING THE FINANCIAL CAPABILITY OF ELEMENTARY SCHOOL STUDENTS

A RESEARCH STUDY AND GUIDANCE

EDUCATION IN A COMPETITIVE AND GLOBALIZING WORLD

Additional books in this series can be found on Nova's website under the Series tab.

Additional e-books in this series can be found on Nova's website under the e-book tab.

EDUCATION IN A COMPETITIVE AND GLOBALIZING WORLD

IMPROVING THE FINANCIAL CAPABILITY OF ELEMENTARY SCHOOL STUDENTS

A RESEARCH STUDY AND GUIDANCE

LAWRENCE RODRIGUEZ
EDITOR

nova publishers
New York

Additional color graphics may be available in the e-book version of this book.

Library of Congress Cataloging-in-Publication Data

ISBN: 978-1-63483-045-4

Published by Nova Science Publishers, Inc. † New York

CONTENTS

PREFACE

Programs and policies designed to promote higher levels of financial capability among youth have proliferated in recent years in the aftermath of the recent economic crisis. This trend is fueled by the growing recognition that more must be done to equip young people with the knowledge, skills and attitudes that will serve as the basis for a lifetime of sound financial decision-making. The recent Executive Order establishing the President's Advisory Council on Financial Capability for Young Americans and the recent announcement of the Financial Literacy Education Commission's (FLEC) new strategic focus on "Starting Early for Financial Success" are both significant markers of increased levels of commitment and dedication among national policy makers to this important issue. This book examines the findings from the Assessing Financial Capability Outcomes (AFCO) Youth Pilot, and provides options and ways to save and invest for students.

In: Improving the Financial Capability … ISBN: 978-1-63483-045-4
Editor: Lawrence Rodriguez

Chapter 1

FINANCIAL EDUCATION AND ACCOUNT ACCESS AMONG ELEMENTARY STUDENTS: FINDINGS FROM THE ASSESSING FINANCIAL CAPABILITY OUTCOMES (AFCO) YOUTH PILOT*

Kasey Wiedrich, J. Michael Collins, Laura Rosen and Ida Rademacher

INTRODUCTION

Programs and policies designed to promote higher levels of financial capability among youth have proliferated in recent years in the aftermath of the recent economic crisis. This trend is fueled by the growing recognition that more must be done to equip young people with the knowledge, skills and attitudes that will serve as the basis for a lifetime of sound financial decision-making. The recent Executive Order establishing the President's Advisory Council on Financial Capability for Young Americans and the recent announcement of the Financial Literacy Education Commission's (FLEC) new strategic focus on "Starting Early for Financial Success" are both significant

* This is an edited, reformatted and augmented version of an April 2014 report, prepared under contract by the Corporation for Enterprise Development for the U.S. Department of the Treasury.

markers of increased levels of commitment and dedication among national policy makers to this important issue.

As interest and investment in youth financial capability grows—especially among public officials needing to determine the most cost- effective use of limited taxpayer dollars—it becomes especially critical to pair program innovation with rigorous evaluation in order to amass a solid base of evidence about "what works." Sadly, the existing evaluation literature on the efficacy of financial education is limited and inconclusive, especially for elementary and middle school children.

One program strategy that holds promise as a potentially effective approach for driving measurable improvements in financial capability is school- based banking or "bank- at- school" programs. These programs pair financial education with access to a savings account with either a credit union or a bank, and with opportunities to actively use those accounts on a regular basis at school. These programs afford students the opportunity to gain experience practicing savings and money management behaviors alongside their peers. Leading financial capability researchers hypothesize that programs that provide a combination of financial education, account access and opportunities to actively use the account are more likely to help students make measurable and durable improvements in financial capability than that provide education alone. However, until now there have been few rigorous evaluations of bank at- school programs that could support or refute this hypothesis.

With support from the U.S. Department of the Treasury, Corporation for Enterprise Development (CFED), the Center for Financial Security at the University of Wisconsin-Madison (CFS), and OpportunityTexas[1] partnered with local school districts and financial institutions to explore the impact of financial education and financial access on elementary age children. The Assessing Financial Capability Outcomes (AFCO) project consisted of field studies with 4th and 5th grade students in two school districts—Eau Claire, Wisconsin and Amarillo, Texas—during the 2011- 2012 and 2012- 2013 academic years. This study offers the first rigorous test of the impact of approximately five hours of classroom- based financial education and access to a bank or credit union branch in school, both alone and in combination, on students':

- Financial knowledge
- Financial behavior, i.e., opening and using savings accounts
- Attitudes towards saving and financial institutions

Financial education is predicted to increase students' correct responses on financial knowledge assessments. Students in schools with in-school bank branches may also demonstrate greater knowledge gains compared to students receiving education alone because an account would provide an opportunity to apply learning. Even students in schools with bank or credit union branches *without* accounts may demonstrate increased knowledge levels as the visibility of banking services might increase the perceived relevance of the financial education curriculum. Students with accounts may also be more likely to make net deposits (fewer withdrawals) if exposed to financial education.

Overall, we found that students did increase their financial knowledge after receiving financial education and that the gains in knowledge persisted a year after receiving the lessons. Students that had bank accounts showed stronger effects in terms of changes in learning, and there was also evidence suggesting that the financial education correlated to more active account use. Student attitudes on how easy they found it to save and whether they found banks useful improved as a result of financial education. Separately, having a bank or credit union located in the school is found to increase not only the likelihood a student is banked, but also the degree to which students felt it was easy to save and that banks were useful.

This study is the first rigorous examination of in-school banks and financial education, despite little research overall on impact of financial education, even less on accounts for children, and the emerging interest an occurrence of these interventions. This study offers a valuable contribution to the field, addressing several of the research priorities identified by the Financial Literacy and Education Commission in 2013 for its "Starting Early for Financial Success" Strategic Focus:

- *Identify and evaluate the relationship between financial education and access to and design of high quality financial products.*
- *Evaluate the delivery of financial education for youth and adults in order to identify effective approaches, delivery channels, and other factors (such as the interaction of knowledge, products, and behaviors) that enhance effectiveness.*
- *Identify, evaluate, and build consensus on "key metrics" for financial education/capability, including measures of knowledge, behavior, and well-being.*
- *Identify opportunities and roles for local, state, and federal governments as scalable platforms for financial capability.*

PRIOR STUDIES ON YOUTH FINANCIAL EDUCATION AND ACCOUNT ACCESS

Scores on the national Jump$tart Coalition's biannual test for high school students have been consistently low since its debut in 1998 (McCormick, 2009; Mandell, 2009). In-school financial education may be a tool to improve low levels of youth financial literacy and to reach all youth, including those who have had fewer opportunities to learn about the financial world outside of school than others. Personal finance is included to some extent in the education standards of 46 states (Council for Economic Education, 2012).

Some authors conclude that older students could achieve more cumulative learning if they begin financial education during younger grades (Sosin et al., 1997). Suiter and Meszaros (2005) also point out that younger children could benefit from financial education as they increasingly make independent financial decisions and are subject to encouragement to spend from peers and the media. Appendix F summarizes the few studies focused on youth in middle and elementary schools; these studies are suggestive of positive effects on learning but far from conclusive.

In general developmental psychology suggests that children make great strides in economic understanding between the ages of six and 12, such that children's understanding is "essentially adult" around age 12 (Webley, 2005). Much of the progress children make by age 12 may be attributable to age-related cognitive development, such as acquiring the ability to understand multiple causation or arithmetic (Webley, 2005). However, direct experience and socialization (including teaching) are also important. Grinstein-Weiss et al. (2009) found a correlation between reported parental teaching of money management and higher credit scores of their children later in life.

In-school banking programs such as Save for America, Illinois Bank at School, and independent bank or credit union partnerships with schools offer children the chance to practice managing money with their own accounts (Johnson & Sherraden, 2007). These programs provide a form of experiential education that complements standard financial education and helps expose children of all backgrounds to financial services (Sherraden et al., 2011; Johnson & Sherraden, 2007; Rand & Slay, 2008). Interaction with a savings account may allow for experiential learning, allowing children to reflect upon concrete experiences and test their own concepts and assumptions (Kolb, Boyatzis, and Mainemelis, 1999; Kourilsky & Carlson, 1996). In particular, providing access to a savings account may help reach children who learn better from hands- on practice than a classroom- only approach (Fox & Bar holomae, 1999; Sherraden et al., 2011). Account access may also help motivate learning of financial education content by demonstrating concrete applications of the material (Sherraden et al., 2011; Mandell & Klein, 2007).

Similarly, account ownership may lead to increased financial knowledge. A survey of 312 high school students in Indiana found an association between owning a savings account and higher financial literacy test scores (Valentine & Khayum, 2005), while an online survey of college alumni found an association between owning bank accounts and investment assets and higher investment knowledge and rates of saving (Peng et al., 2007).

Schools and financial institutions are increasingly partnering to offer savings account programs to children from elementary to high school to help complement financial education and instill successful financial habits. As of 2007, 198 high schools, 207 elementary schools, 41 middle schools, two K- 12 schools, and 13 youth centers in 30 states had youth- run credit union branches (Johnson & Sherraden, 2007).

Exposure to banking services could allow children to learn by testing what they know and reflecting upon their experiences. Financial inclusion and financial education could be especially important for children who have had relatively little opportunity to learn about or practice healthy financial behaviors. Additional research is required, however, to causally identify the effects of financial education and access. This field study is designed in part to further understand these issues.

PROGRAM DESIGN

This study began in the 2011- 2012 school year with 4th and 5th grade students in Eau Claire, Wisconsin. Because the sample size was insufficient in the first year of the pilot, we continued the study the next school year with 4th graders in Eau Claire and added a second pilot site with 4th graders in Amarillo, Texas. While there were a small number of differences between the pilots in the two sites as described below, they were similar in design and both included:

- Teacher preparation including in-service trainings and lesson materials;
- Use of standardized curriculum that could be completed in five to six weeks;

- Use of a standardized in school assessment survey on financial knowledge, attitudes, and behaviors;
- Collection of banking usage (for students with accounts);
- A random, staggered design in which classroom- based cohorts received education and others did no
- Access to in-school banking for approximately half of the schools in the school districts;
- For all outcomes, baseline measures were collected before the financial education began and follow-up measures were collected after the financial education was administered.

With the random assignment of the financial education by classroom and varying access to in-school bank and credit union branches, the research design in both sites provides four comparison groups:

	Financial education	**No financial education**
Credit union or bank in school	Credit union or bank in school + financial education	Credit union or bank in school + **No** financial education
No credit union or bank in school	**No** credit union or bank in school + financial education	**No** credit union or bank in school + **No** financial education

Eau Claire, Wisconsin Pilot

During the spring 2 12 semester, all 4th and 5th grade students in the Eau Claire School District participated in a five- lesson classroom financial education program called Money F- I- T. Half the district's classrooms were randomly assigned to participate in the program during the study period ("treatment"), and the remaining classrooms participated immediately after the study's follow- up assessment had been completed ("controls"), as the school district wanted all of the students to receive the financial education. All students were given an assessment (see Appendix H) prior to the start of the financial education program (the "study period") started, and again after the program ended (before the "control group" teachers began teaching the program). The same design was used during the spring 2013 semester when the pilot continued with the new 4th grade class. Implementing the study for a second year in Eau Claire created an opportunity to follow- up with 2012 4th graders almost a year later as 5th graders, after all students had received financial education. Students were administered the assessment a third time, allowing us to examine the persistence on any affects we see in the first year.

The Money F- I- T curriculum was adapted from the Council on Economic Education's Financial Fitness for Life curriculum, drawing primarily from the lessons addressing savings, financial decision- making, and money management (see Appendix D for an overview of the lessons). The curriculum was delivered in five lessons of approximately 45- minutes each. To ensure fidelity of treatment and collect teachers' perspectives of the lessons, teachers were asked to provide feedback after each lesson was taught in their classroom. Overall, teacher feedback on the lessons was quite positive. The teachers reported that the material was appropriate for the students' learning level and held their interest. Importantly, most teachers felt that students had not previously studied the material and that the lessons were a valuable addition to the curriculum.

Teachers attended a 3- hour training session during a professional development in-service day, and were compensated $100 for time spent preparing for lessons outside the normal work day. In some cases volunteers from Royal Credit Union were used to teach the curriculum due to other demands on teachers' time. The training session was intended to standardize the financial education treatment.[2]

Approximately half of the schools in the study also had access to in school banking. Royal Credit Union (RCU) is based in Eau Claire and has 21 offices, 120,000 members, and over $1 billion in assets, making it one of the largest credit unions in the area. RCU began a program called School $ense in 1993 at the request of an elementary school principal, and it has since grown to more than two dozen schools. School $ense operated student branches in six of the Eau Claire school district's 13 elementary schools during the study.

Modeled after the Save for America program, School $ense allows children and a parent or guardian (joint member) to op n a savings account with RCU, which furnishes the required $5 initial deposit (see Appendix C). Joint members must apply online or in-person at RCU offices to open the account, but from then on children can make deposits and withdrawals at school. School branches are operated at least once a week and are set up as tables outside the cafeteria. Teachers collect deposits from their students and deliver them to the mobile branch table. Deposits can be of any amount, and elementary school students can withdraw up to $20 at a time with a joint member's signature.[3] Students are encouraged to identify a savings goal and to track progress toward that goal. Students can also earn small prizes, earned for every fourth deposit. Student tellers (4th and 5th graders) process the deposits with RCU staff at lunchtime. These tellers are hired through a true- to- life process; students fill out an application and interview for a position.

During the study period, students in schools with RCU branches had weekly opportunities to access their accounts. This provided multiple opportunities for students to be exposed to accounts or make deposits and withdrawals over the course of the spring term.

Each school has two or three classes per grade, with approximately 1,500 4th and 5th graders total in the district in the 2011- 2012 school year. To enroll students in the study, students had to sign assent forms, and their parent or guardian had to sign a parental consent form to allow the study to use individual assessment data and to release credit union account data, if the student had an account. Numerous messaging strategies were used to inform parents about study recruitment, including brochures, fliers, and letters sent home with students, school newsletter articles, emails sent directly to parents, and local media coverage. However, consent in the baseline year was lower than expected, with only 569 students in the final sample (about 38%, fully 10 percentage points lower than anticipated). This small sample necessitated the continuation of the pilot for a second year with the new 4th grade class, with approximately 760 students, and the selection of a second school district to participate in the pilot.

Amarillo, Texas Pilot

Amarillo, Texas was selected as the second site for the pilot as it offered a larger school district with a supportive administration and a local financial institution with existing in-school banking programs. Amarillo also offered a more diverse setting to test the interventions; the Eau Claire School District's students were 81% white in 2011- 2012 in contrast to only 38% of students in Amarillo (see Appendix B). There are 36 elementary schools in the Amarillo Independent School District, with approximately 2,500 4th graders total in the district. During the spring 2013 semester, 4th grade students in Amarillo participated in an educational program similar to Money F- I- T called *Smarter Texans Save*. Half the district's teachers were randomly assigned to participate in the program during the study period, and the remaining teachers participated after the study period.[4] *Smarter Texans Save* consisted of six, weekly 45-minute lessons delivered by the students' regular classroom math teachers over a five week period. All students were given an assessment prior to the start of the financial education program and again after the program ended.

The *Smarter Texans Save* curriculum was also adapted from the Financial Fitness for Life curriculum and largely matched the Money F- I- T curriculum. Some adjustments were made to the curriculum and the student assessment so that they covered the majority of the new grade 4 math personal finance curriculum standards that are part of the new K- 8 personal financial curriculum standards the Texas legislature passed in 2011. Texas school districts are not required to teach the new standards until the 2014- 2015 school year, so this pilot provided an early opportunity to test and get feedback on the new curriculum standards in one school district.

Teachers attended a 6- hour training session and were compensated up to $90 for time spent preparing for lessons outside the normal work day and providing feedback on each lesson.[5] Each lesson was documented by the instructor to verify what education took place and when. Overall, teachers reported that they were satisfied with the lessons and felt that their students were learning the concepts, retaining them and applying them in later lessons. They also were surprised at how much the students enjoyed and understood the lessons. One teacher reported that, "we have had some rich discussions about savings and budgeting since doing these lessons. The fixed and variable expenses were eye openers for my students…and have helped them relate to the struggles their families go through."

In addition to the overall positive feedback, two primary themes emerged from teachers' feedback: students' level of understanding and teacher preparedness. A number of teachers reported that their students' initial level of understanding of the vocabulary and concepts used in lessons was very limited, which teachers felt was due to students' limited previous exposure to the concepts, particularly English Language Learner students. A few teachers reported that the concept of savings was non existent to their students before the lessons. However, teachers reported that after really working with students who struggled with the concepts, their students understood them by the end of the lesson. In particular, teachers believed that students developed an understanding of the value of savings. Teachers expressed concern about the material's relevance for students at all income levels. For example, one teacher questioned referencing trips to Disneyland with student who may not have taken a vacation, and another believed that her students would have done better on a lesson if "more of their parents had checking accounts. Several of [her students'] parents cash their checks at a local store, not a bank." Regarding teacher preparedness, teachers felt they were prepared to teach the lessons and said that the training had been helpful. Each lesson was taught to teachers during the teacher training, which teachers reported was helpful to experience the lesson through the eyes of their students.

As in Eau Claire, half of the schools in the district also had access to an in-school banking program. Happy State Bank (HSB) is a Texas- based community bank with 31 locations, 69,000 accounts and $2 billion in total assets. HSB started its Kids' Bank program in 1997 at Sleepy Hollow Elementary School in Amarillo. The program has since expanded to 30 schools in 9 communities in the Texas Panhandle. The Kids' Bank program allows children and a parent or responsible party to open a joint savings account with HSB with no minimum balance requirements (see Appendix C). For this pilot, children were also allowed to open accounts in their name only without the signature of their parents, if the parents lacked the documentation required to open the account.[6] Once the account has been established, children can make deposits at the school, or they can go to any HSB location to make deposits or withdrawals.

Kids' Bank student branches were operating in three of Amarillo's 36 elementary schools prior to the study's implementation. As part of the study, the Kids' Bank program was expanded to 15 *additional* schools within the Amarillo Independent School District, with selected schools chosen at random, so that during the study period 18 schools within the district participated in the banking program, and 18 did not.[7] After the study period, schools that were not randomly selected to enroll in the Kids' Bank program were given the opportunity to do so. The 15 schools that were randomly selected to open Kids' Banks were also given the option to end their involvement following the study period, but, with the encouragement of the district's superintendent, the majority elected to continue the in-school branches. The teachers also provided feedback on the Kids' Bank programs and how the in-school branches enhanced the financial education lessons. The feedback was nearly all positive, and teachers reported that their students were excited about saving and one said that her students looked forward to their bank day. Teachers also believed that the students' participation in the Kids' Bank brought concepts taught in the financial education lessons to life. One teacher reported that students with accounts seem more involved in the lessons as they understood that the lesson is relevant to them.

Due to the rapid and high-volume expansion of the Kids' Bank program into Amarillo for the pilot, many of the normal features of the Kids' Bank were omitted from the program during the study period. As in the RCU School $ense model, HSB hires students to work at the Kids' Banks in cooperation with banking professionals, but there was not sufficient time to hire and train student tellers. HSB officers were solely responsible for running the Kids' Bank programs at the selected schools. Typically each school is encouraged to utilize and promote the program in a way that is most beneficial for their campus, but due to the number of Kids' Banks being opened and the need for uniformity during the study, the 15 new schools all used a similar model and program design. The Kids' Bank branch is set up in a public area of the school, and during the study period, the branches were open once a week in each school. Each school's administration select the time of day for students to make deposits – either before school, at lunch or after school. Each time a child makes a deposit into their account, he or she receives a prize from the treasure chest as an incentive to save. Schools actively promote the Kids' Bank program to their students, and often send home flyers or other information about the program to parents.

A significant difference between the pilots in Eau Claire and Amarillo was the length of most students' exposure to the in-school banking programs. As stated above, RCU's School $ence was a well- established program in the Eau Claire elementary schools, and a significant number of students were banked prior to the pilot's implementation. In Amarillo, only three of the schools had existing Kids' Bank branches, so the pilot represented the first exposure to bank accounts in school for the majority of students. Due to the short timeframe we had to plan and implement the pilot, the Kids' Bank branches rolled out approximately two weeks prior to the start of the *Smarter Texans Save* lessons. In order to increase the number of students who had HSB accounts during the study period, we randomly selected students within banked schools to receive a $25 seed deposit if they opened a Kids' Bank account.[8] Approximately half of students in banked schools were selected to receive the incentive through drawings held in their math classrooms. This was done at the request of teachers and the school district's administration, who wanted the process of selecting incentive offer recipients to be transparent to students.

The new Kids' Bank programs launched in the schools in January 2013, and by the end of the school year, 415 4th grade students opened new accounts with HSB, 38% of the students in schools with new in-school branches.[9] The take- up of account varied considerably by school, with only 20% of students opening accounts in one school up to 60% of students in another. A variety of factors likely affected student account take- up. Because the school's assistant principal or principal was responsible for implementing the program at their school, their level of commitment to the program seemed to be a primary factor affecting account take- up. While assistant principals' and teachers' capacity to support the bank- at- school program varied, the majority of school leadership and nearly all teachers had positive feedback about the program. Another factor appeared to be the level of commitment from the two bank employees assigned to each campus had towards the program. Two schools with high take- up rates had bank employees that were very engaged with the program. At one of these schools, the bank employee made a mural about the Kids' Bank in the school's entryway. Finally, the time of day the Kids' Bank took place may have impacted student participation. Principals could elect to have the Kids' Bank take place before school, during lunch or after school. Some principals reported that they had greater student participation when the Kids' Bank took place after school.

It was also observed that, on average, schools with a higher percentage of economically disadvantaged students had higher account take- up. Five of the six schools with the highest account take- up had over 83% economically disadvantaged students during the 2011- 2012 school year, while the average percentage of economically disadvantaged students in schools with new Kids' Banks was 79%.[10] At one school with a high percentage of economically disadvantaged and Hispanic students, the assistant principal attributed her school's high account take- up to the parents of her school's predominately Hispanic students who are "all about their kids." She said that her students' parents seemed proud that they had taken advantage of the opportunity to open a savings account for their child, particularly because some of her students' parents likely didn't have a checking or savings account themselves. A number of her students' parents participated in the program, making deposits with their child after school. Another principal at a school with a high percentage of economically disadvantaged students was impressed with how many of [her] students were depositing money even though they may not have a lot of money at home."

Like in Wisconsin, parental consent for was necessary for students' enrollment in the study, and consent forms were sent home with students and could be returned to school or mailed back, with a follow up mailing to those parents that didn't initially respond. Instead of written student assent, verbal student assent to be included in the study was requested prior to the administration of the pre-assessment. A communications and marketing campaign was implemented prior to the study, involving a press release and local media coverage to build awareness and legitimacy around the study. Numerous messaging strategies were used to inform parents about study recruitment, including brochures and letters sent home with students, school newsletter articles, social media and automated phone messages left with parents about the study.

DATA COLLECTION

The data collected for this study include a baseline survey of the students before the financial education began, a second survey after the financial education was completed, and administrative data from partner financial institutions. The survey includes a 13- point financial literacy quiz, and other questions to measure student attitudes, beliefs, and experiences with financial issues. The follow- up and baseline quiz questions are identical, making the difference of the changes in quiz scores between the treatment and control groups the measure of interest. Financial attitudes and behaviors are captured through questions such as how often the student saves money, how important they believe it is, and how difficult they find it (see Appendix H). RCU and HSB each provided transactional data for students with bank or credit union accounts whose parents consented to share data. Non- assenting students and students whose parents did not sign consent forms still received the financial education and completed the surveys but are not included in this analysis.

Table 1. Sample Size by Data Source

	Eau Claire		Amarillo		Total	
	Baseline	**Follow -up**	**Baseline**	**Follow-up**	**Baseline**	**Follow-up**
Survey	745	710	756	723	1501	1,433
Bank Data		270		166		436

Students were randomized into the education and control groups by classroom. Table 2 below shows the sample size by treatment group for the students that consented to participate in the study and completed both surveys.

Table 2. Sample Size by Treatment Group

	Eau Claire	Amarillo	Total
No Financial Education	320	285	605
Financial Education	380	418	798
Total	700	703	1,403

In both school districts, some schools have bank branches on campus and others do not. A total of 715 students had in school banking access and 664 did not. These in-school banks were not all randomly assigned so differences among students in the two groups may reflect any inherent differences in the population that attracted a bank to one school and not another. As the table below shows, students with a bank branch in school are much more likely (64.3% vs. 39.9%, or 24 percentage points) to report having a bank account (as reported in the survey).

There are consistent differences at baseline both between students with and without bank accounts, and between students with and without bank branches in their school. The students with bank accounts and in school access exhibit greater financial literacy quiz scores at baseline, and more positive opinions about banks. It should be noted that according to 2011- 2012 statistics, 67% of the students in Amarillo schools were eligible for free or reduced price lunch, compared to 41% in Eau Claire. This might suggest the two school districts offer two differing contexts for the availability of financial education and access, although the median income and overall poverty level are similar in the two communities (see Appendix B).

Table 3. Banking Access and Student Reporting being Banked

	Bank in School	No Bank in School	Total
Student Banked	460 (64.3%)	265 (39.9%)	725 (52.6%)
Student Unbanked	255	399	654
Total	715	664	1379

Table 4. Baseline Differences by Bank in School Status

	Eau Claire				Amarillo			
	Student Banked	Student Unbanked	Bank in School	No Bank in School	Student Banked	Student Unbanked	Bank in School	No Bank in School
Quiz Score	6.7	5.8	6.4	6.0	5.8	5.3	5.7	5.4
Banks Useful to You (5pt)	4.0	3.6	4.0	3.7	4.0	3.7	4.0	3.7
Count	467	209	408	268	258	445	307	396

Table 5. Eau Claire Second Year Sample Size by Data Source

	Eau Claire
Survey	277
Bank Data	121

All data from Amarillo were collected in the spring of 2013, while the Eau Claire sample comes from both spring 2012 and spring 2013. As stated above, conducting the pilot for a second year in Eau Claire created an opportunity to follow- up with 2012 4th graders almost a year later as 5th graders, after all students had received financial education. These data can help us understand the persistence on any affects we see in the first year.

ANALYSIS

This study is based on a selected number of outcomes predicted to change in response to the intervention. These include:

- **Financial Quiz Score:** The number of questions students answer correctly out of 13 questions.
- **Banked:** Students' report whether or not they have a bank account in their own name (where "do not know" is considered "no").
- **Spend Money Immediately:** Students' report on a 5- point scale how often they find it hard to avoid spending money immediately.
- **Easy to Save:** Students' report on a 5- point scale how often they find it easy to save money.
- **Saving is for Adults:** Students report on a 5- point scale how often they feel that saving money is only for adults.
- **Banks Useful to You:** Students' report on a 5- point scale the degree to which they believe that banks offer services that are useful to them.
- **Net Deposits:** Administrative data from partner financial institutions on the total amount of money that is deposited into the account net of the total withdrawn from the account.
- **Active Account Use:** Administrative data on the number of distinct occasions on which money is deposited or withdrawn from the account.

The results shown in this report are based on statistical regressions used to estimate the change in outcomes of interest from baseline to follow- up. Reported coefficients can be interpreted as the "amount of change" for each outcome. Most models are Ordinary Least Squares (OLS), except banked status, which uses a Probit model, and the number of deposits and withdrawals which use a Poisson (count) model. All models use clustered standard errors at the classroom level for the Eau Claire students because it is the level at which the treatment is applied, and at the school level in Amarillo because classroom information is not available. Most models include two control variables measured at baseline: (1) a 5- item index measuring how well the student performs in school (scale reliability coefficient=.71) and (2) a 4- item index measuring how much they believe financial issues are only the responsibility of their parents (scale reliability coefficient=.61). Each composite index is derived from baseline survey questions.

Bank data are available for 166 students in Amarillo and 270 students in Eau Claire. The bank data includes transactions students made from October 2012 through June 2013 for Eau Claire, and January 2013 through June 2013 for Amarillo. The data form a panel of weekly bank activity including net deposits, number of transactions, and banked status. The exposure to financial education occurred over time; as such the education treatment variable is defined as the number of financial education lessons a given student would have received by a given week, scaled between 0 and 1 by units of 1/6 so the regression coefficients represent the effect of the entire 6- lesson education curriculum. Estimates are based on student/account fixed effects regressions to determine the effect of receiving an additional financial education lesson.

Each estimate included in these tables begins with the average effects of the financial education curriculum (the column labeled "Direct Effect"). Next an interaction between a student who received financial education and having in-school banking is introduced to measure the degree to which the financial education has a different effect when it is combined with bank account access ("Int: Bank in School"). The next column interacts receiving financial education and the student being banked at baseline to measure the degree to which the financial education has a different effect on students that have bank accounts ("Int: Banked").

There are several additional variations related to the banking data estimates. A subset of students in Amarillo was randomly assigned to receive a

$25 incentive to open a bank account at an in-school branch. This allows an estimation of the effects of this incentive to open an account at the student level. The randomly drawn incentive money can serve as an instrument for whether or not the student opens a new bank account. The "seed money lottery" coefficient reflects the effects of the incentive and bank branch relative to students who only have access to the bank branch.

To provide a benchmark for the treatment effects, the table below shows baseline means of the outcome variables across the two study sites. The average financial knowledge score is 5.84 out of 13. About half (53%) of students are reported to be banked. The remaining items are drawn from 5-point scale questions about relative agreement levels.

Table 6. Summary Statistics: Student Assessment Surveys

Outcome	Count	Mean	Standard Deviation
Quiz Score (13pt)	1501	5.84	2.33
Banked (per survey)	1472	52.6%	0.50
Spend Money Immediately (5pt)	1466	2.77	1.17
Easy to Save (5pt)	1468	3.59	1.12
Saving is for Adults (5pt)	1501	1.76	1.07
Banks Useful to You (5pt)	1467	3.87	1.11

The table below shows summary statistics for the *weekly* bank account observations. Among those with accounts that could be matched and used in this analysis, the average deposits were around $6.90 in Eau Claire and $0.80 in Amarillo. About 7% of Amarillo students made a deposit each week; 28% of Eau Claire students did so. Because the bank activity is different between Eau Claire and Amarillo, banking results are displayed separately by school district.

Table 7. Summary Statistics: Bank Administrative Data[11]

	Amarillo		**Eau Claire**	
	Mean	**St Dev**	**Mean**	**St Dev**
Net Deposits ($)	0.8	6.8	6.9	285.8
Weekly Transactions (% of students)	0.07	0.27	0.28	0.59

Knowledge Gains

Financial education appears to produce a large improvement in financial knowledge—an increase in the number of correct questions between 1.8 and 2.0. This is close to a full standard deviation unit (a 0.77 effect size). There is no evidence that having a bank branch in the school has an added effect on learning during the study period. In the absence of financial education, students who were banked before the program do improve their scores more than the unbanked, but students who receive the financial education come close to catching up or surpassing the banked students with the education. These results are in the table below and also shown as means in the figure.

Table 8. Regression Results: Financial Quiz Score

	Direct Effects	**Int: Bank in School**	**Int: Banked**	**All Interactions**
Financial Education	1.774***	1.680***	2.069***	1.962***
	(0.000)	(0.000)	(0.000)	(0.000)
Bank in School	-0.0213	-0.123	-0.0138	-0.261
	(0.893)	(0.578)	(0.930)	(0.369)
Student Was Banked	0.346**	0.343**	0.665***	0.649**
	(0.007)	(0.007)	(0.000)	(0.008)
Bank and Education		0.179		0.253
		(0.571)		(0.552)
Education and Student Banked			-0.563*	-0.719*
			(0.015)	(0.027)
Bank in School and Student Banked				0.110
				(0.746)
Fin Ed and Bank in School and Student				0.156
Banked				
				(0.736)
Observations	1374	1374	1374	1374

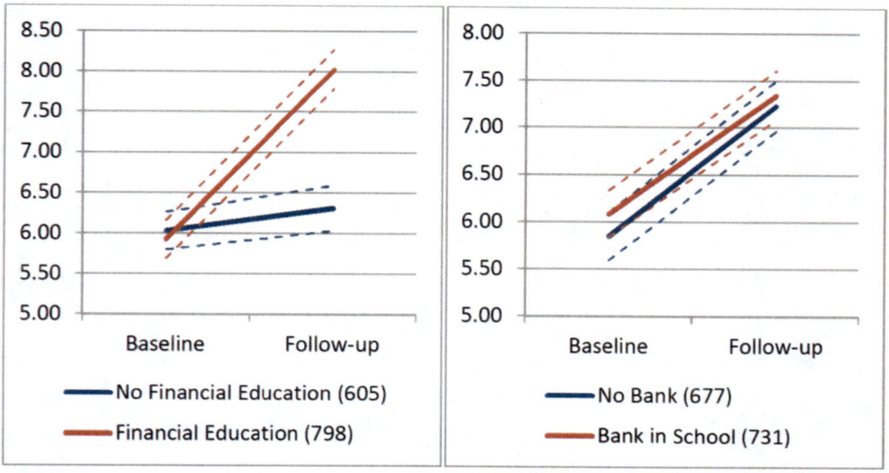

Figure 1. Financial Quiz Score.

The following tables breaks out estimates by school district, showing greater gains in number of correct questions in Amarillo (2.25) than Eau Claire (1.3). Neither program shows statistically significant or positive effects of schools having banking services on site in terms of knowledge gains. The effects of being banked on knowledge gains were more pronounced in Amarillo.

Table 9. Regression Results: Financial Quiz Score by Site

	Direct (WI)	Direct (TX)	Int: Bank in School (WI)	Int: Bank in School (TX)	Int: Banked (WI)	Int: Banked (TX)
Financial Education	1.322***	2.251***	0.985***	2.179***	1.924***	2.175***
	(0.000)	(0.000)	(0.000)	(0.000)	(0.000)	(0.000)
Bank in School	-0.0285	-0.0735	-0.329	-0.170	-0.00645	-0.0728
	(0.895)	(0.721)	(0.196)	(0.551)	(0.976)	(0.724)
Student was Banked	0.0912	0.446**	0.0752	0.446**	0.553	0.320
	(0.658)	(0.009)	(0.717)	(0.009)	(0.060)	(0.164)

Table 9. (Continued)

Bank and Education			0.553	0.162		
			(0.161)	(0.699)		
Education and Student					-0.875*	0.208
Banked						
					(0.020)	(0.473)
Observations	671	703	671	703	671	703

The average treatment effects of education on financial knowledge are strongly positive in both Eau Claire and Amarillo. However, these average gains may result from some schools experiencing large gains that cover for other schools that see little or no benefit. A school administrator contemplating a financial education program will likely be interested in the probability his or her school will be among those that benefit. The figure below plots average baseline and follow- up quiz scores for treatment and control students w thin each school. Every point above the 45 degree line represents a gain in knowledge. Virtually all the largest gains come from treated students. Only two schools failed to experience gains for their treated students, whereas the control students are much more balance between increases and decreased in measured knowledge.

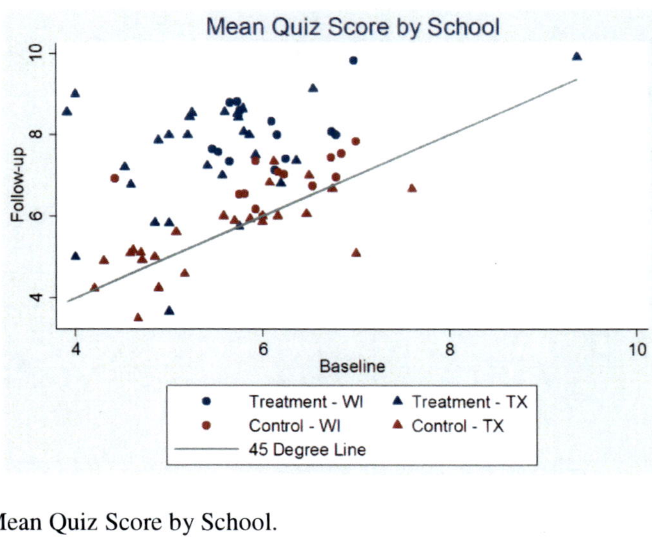

Figure 2. Mean Quiz Score by School.

Banking

The banked/unbanked status of each student was measured as part of the assessment at start and end of the study. Table 10 below shows that financial education is associated with students reporting having a bank account at follow up who did not have any account at the start of the project. The marginal estimate is that education increases the number of banked students by about 3.5%.[12] Somewhat surprisingly, the effects were not more pronounced if a student had access to a bank at school.

Looking only at the 307 students in Amarillo at schools where bank accounts were offered, the students who were randomly selected for a $25 incentive causes about an 18.1% marginal increase in students obtaining accounts who previously did not have them. However, there are not stronger effects based on an interaction of receiving an incentive to open an account and education.

Table 11 shows that the effect of having a bank in school on unbanked students becoming banked is predominately found in Eau Claire. This is likely because the credit union branches are long established and the education served as a trigger for students to seek out an account. In Amarillo, the majority of in-school bank branches were new and students' understanding of their ability to open account was based on a shorter term exposure.

Table 10. Regression Results: Student Banked

	Fin Ed	Int: Bank in School	Seed Money	Int: Seed Money
Financial Education	0.0338*	0.0316	0.0454	0.0726
	(0.018)	(0.065)	(0.191)	(0.120)
Bank & Education		0.00452		
		(0.875)		
Seed Money Lottery			0.181***	0.223**
			(0.000)	(0.004)
Education & Lottery				-0.074
				(0.376)
Observations	1359	1359	307	307

Note: marginal effects reported.

Table 11. State-Specific Regression Results: Student Banked

	Fin Ed (WI)	Fin Ed (TX)	Int: Bank in School (WI)	Int: Bank in School (TX)
Financial Education	0.0474*	0.0274	0.0621*	0.0151
	(0.013)	(0.122)	(0.026)	(0.378)
Bank and Education			-0.0282	0.0267
			(0.447)	(0.509)
Observations	657	702	657	702

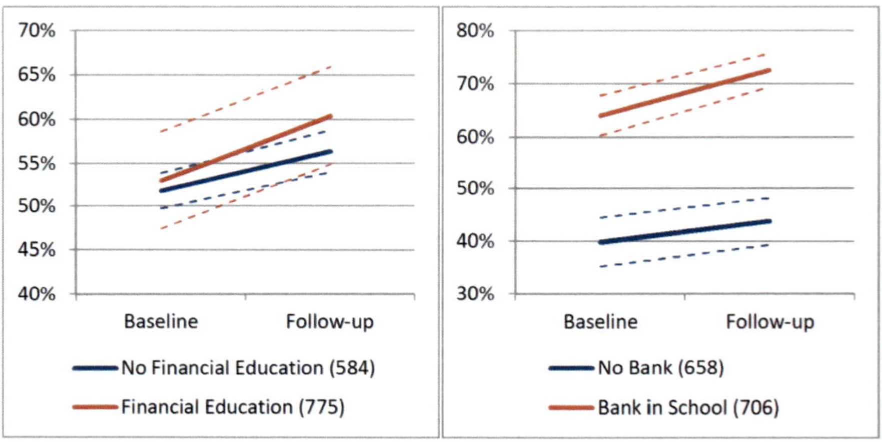

Figure 3. Banking Status of Student.

Figure 4 shows the students without financial education also experienced an increase in becoming banked. Further analysis shows much of this increase comes from students with on- campus bank branches.

Deposits

Data on each account held by a student was available for 270 students in Eau Claire (Table 12) and 166 students in Amarillo (Table 13). The main results include month fixed effects to capture any seasonal trends in bank activity. The second column in each table omits the month fixed effects as a robustness check.[13]

The next column shows the effects of education in school with banks than in schools without in-school branches. These models are not applicable in Amarillo because virtually all bank data comes from students with bank branches in school. Finally the last column, provided only in Table 12 for Eau Claire, takes advantage of the fact that some students in Eau Claire had accounts even though their school lacked a credit union branch. This permits an analysis of deposits by students with in-school branches to see if they appear different from that of students in schools without in-school branches. (In Amarillo all bank data comes from students with branches in school.)

None of these coefficients are statistically significant, but the estimates are positive for financial education. That is, net deposits were higher on average (by about $7.69) after education and higher for students after education with banking access. The overall findings cannot confirm stronger effects of the financial education on net deposits based upon the presence of the bank in school. Net deposits is a relatively noisy measure at the weekly level, and with only 270 students, it is difficult to estimate results that are statistically significant.

Figure 5 below shows average weekly deposits in Eau Claire for all students. Even after smoothing the data with a 3- week moving average, the graph highlights the "noisy" nature of the data. The shaded region represents the six- week period when the financial education was delivered. Since the treatment and control groups received financial education during different periods in the semester, each week depicted in this figure is taken from two different calendar weeks in order to make the timing of the financial education coincide. Note that the median net deposit is zero in every week, which indicates the averages are strongly influenced by the tails of the distribution.

Table 12. Eau Claire Regression Results: Net Deposits

	Main	No Month Effects	Interaction	Bank
Financial Education	7.689	16.68		
	(0.542)	(0.056)		
Fin Ed (with Bank)			10.45	
			(0.513)	
Fin Ed (without Bank)			-0.212	
			(0.990)	
Bank in School				2.128
				(0.504)

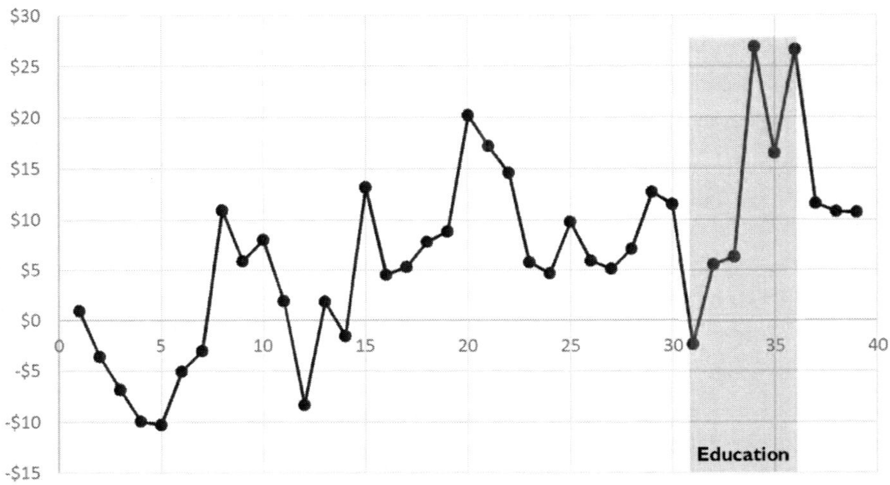

Figure 4. Net Deposits by Week - Eau Claire 3-Week Moving Average ($).

The estimated effects for Amarillo are statistically significant, but the opposite of what would be predicted in terms of financial education increasing net deposits. Financial education is associated with *lower* net deposits by about $1.10 on average. One explanation could be the lottery payments used as an incentive for opening an account could potentially be withdrawn. However, students who were selected for the $25 seed incentive payment and who received education show positive estimates for net deposits, not at statistically significant levels, suggesting that students were not withdrawing the seed deposit. The Amarillo sample was smaller than Eau Claire, which further limits statistical power. Overall these results are not conclusive that education boosts deposit activity.

Table 13. Amarillo Regression Results: Net Deposits

	Main	No Month Effects	Interaction
Financial Education	-1.096*	-1.508***	-1.849**
	(0.036)	(0.000)	(0.009)
Seed Money	0.623	1.239***	0.308
	(0.147)	(0.000)	(0.507)
Fin Ed and Seed Money			1.176
			(0.121)

The figure below shows average weekly deposits in Amarillo for all students, similarly adjusted as Figure 5 above to make the timing of the financial education coincide for the treatment and control groups. The deposits are much smaller and less variable in Amarillo compared to Eau Claire. Also, there is a general downward trend in deposits as opposed to the upward trend observed in Eau Claire, which may be due in part to the fact that the Kids' Banks were not available weekly in each school following the treatment period and some schools chose to end the in-school branches before the end of the school year. As in Eau Claire, the median net deposit in Amarillo is zero every week.

Another outcome of interest is students simply becoming more active account users. The active account indicator signals students who use their account regularly. Eau Claire students must use the account 4 times to qualify (65% of students with accounts) and students in Amarillo must use the account 3 times to qualify (15% of students with accounts).

Table 14 and 15 show the results of students being active account users as a marginal effect based on probit regressions. Having an in-school branch is strongly associated with an increased probability that a student will use his or her account at least 4 times. There are no significant effects associated with education or combinations of education and accounts.

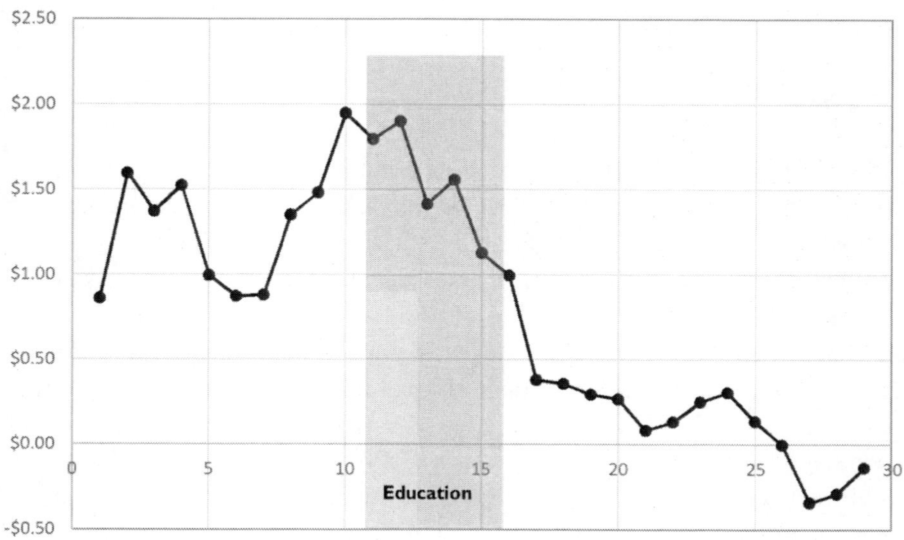

Figure 5. Net Deposits by Week – Amarillo 3-Week Moving Average ($).

Table 14. Eau Claire Regression Results: Active Accounts

	Main	No Month Effects	Interaction	Bank
Financial Education	0.00568	0.00129		-0.0791
	(0.588)	(0.836)		(0.700)
Fin Ed (with Bank)			0.0126	
			(0.328)	
Fin Ed (without Bank)			-0.0137	
			(0.364)	
Bank in School				0.455*
				(0.011)

Table 15 shows the similar estimates for Amarillo. Here financial education is associated with students being more active account users, at least when monthly fixed effects are excluded from the estimates. The intera tion between being offered $25 to open an account and education is negative, however. Again this may be an artifact of students spending down the incentive, making one or two withdraws and no additional deposits. These results are suggestive but do not offer strong, statistically significant effects on active bank account use associated with education.

Attitudes

In addition to knowledge and banking behavior, financial education also has the potential to influence student s attitudes about saving and financial institutions. Both the Eau Claire and Amarillo studies included attitude questions in pre-and post- program assessments, allowing for estimates of changing attitudes over the course of the study period. Table 16 summarizes the results for 4 questions, each on a 5- point scale.[14] Only two showed significant coefficients, Easy to save (How often do you find it easy to save money?) and Banks useful to you (Do you think banks and credit unions provide services that are useful to you?). Both showed positive effects of education and having a branch in school, with strongest effects from financial education on attitudes towards banks/credit unions.

Table 15. Amarillo Regression Results: Active Accounts

	Main	No Month Effects	Interaction
Financial Education	0.0506	0.109*	0.108
	(0.453)	(0.036)	(0.221)
Seed Money	-0.0468	0.0508	0.000215
	(0.361)	(0.098)	(0.996)
Fin Ed and Seed Money			-0.0893*
			(0.026)

Table 16. Education and Bank Effects on Financial Attitudes in Student Survey

	Spend money immediately (5pt)	Easy to save (5pt)	Saving is for adults (5pt)	Banks useful to you (5pt)
Financial Education	-0.0542	0.0956*	-0.0617	0.173***
	(0.274)	(0.011)	(0.060)	(0.000)
Bank in School	-0.0440	0.102*	0.00222	0.112**
	(0.427)	(0.030)	(0.955)	(0.006)
Observations	1345	1349	1372	1341

Figure 7 shows the means for the perception of saving variable over time. Financial education produces a modest increase in all students' perceptions of how easy it is to save money. In Amarillo, the students who opened accounts in response to the $25 seed funds showed a very large increase in perceived ability to save, but the estimate is not statistically significant. There is no evidence of other interaction effects between in-school banks, students being banked, and education.

Figure 8 displays results for the question about the usefulness of banks and credit unions. Financial education clearly increases how much students believe banks offer services that are useful to them. Unlike many of the other outcomes where treatment effects are due to financial education producing larger gains, the control group was flat on this outcome over the study.

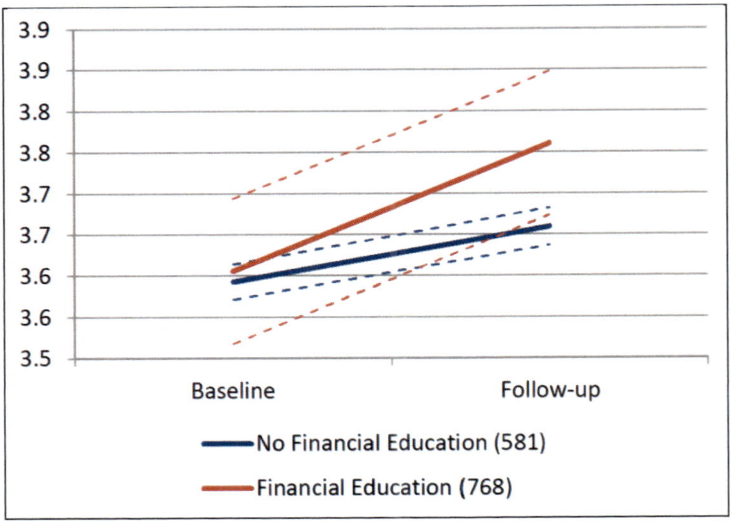

Figure 6. Easy To Save (5 Pt Scale).

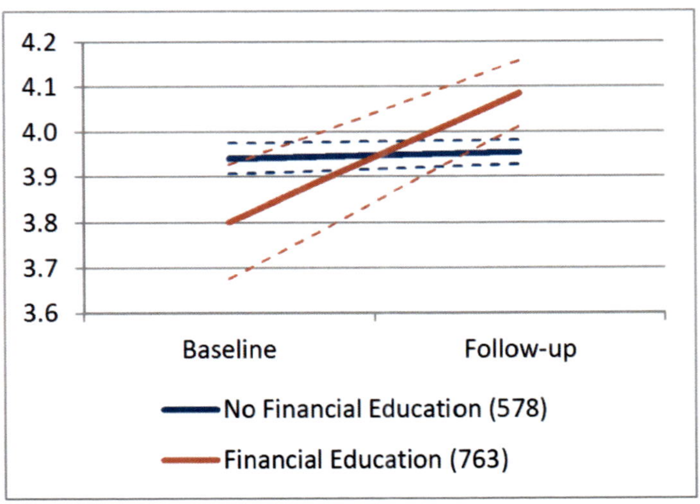

Figure 7. Banks Are Useful to You (5pt).

Table 17 displays more detailed analysis of the findings in the figure above. The effect on changes in attitudes about banks is almost entirely driven by the financial education, with some stronger effects related to having a bank in school combined with education. The student actually being banked is negative but not significant. Receiving the $25 seed money lottery (in Amarillo) combined with education is positive, but not statistically significant.

Table 17. Regression Results: Banks Are Useful to You (5pt)

	Fin Ed	Int: Bank in School	Int: Banked	Seed Money	Int: Seed Money	Int: New Acct
Financial Education	0.170***	0.102	0.219***	0.176**	0.130	-0.0235
	(0.000)	(0.067)	(0.000)	(0.005)	(0.320)	(0.914)
Bank and Education		0.133*				
		(0.047)				
Education and Student Was Banked			-0.0957			
			(0.156)			
Seed Money Lottery				0.0662	0.0185	
				(0.542)	(0.440)	
Education and Lottery					0.0821	
					(0.666)	
Student becomes Banked						0.191
						(0.805)
Education and Student becomes Banked						0.297
						(0.361)
Observations	1341	1341	1337	296	296	296

The next table (18) shows the effects by site. The main effect of financial education is more than twice as large in Amarillo than Eau Claire, but both are large and significant. Financial education provided at a school with an onsite branch shows larger effects, at least in Eau Claire. The interaction effects for the student being banked at the outset show a negative coefficient, which implies that the education effect is mainly among students who were un anked.

The estimate for the interaction for Amarillo was not significant, but the main effect of education persists.

Table 18. Site-Specific Regression Results: Banks Useful to You

	Fin Ed (WI)	Fin Ed (TX)	Int: Bank in School (WI)	Int: Bank in School (TX)	Int: Banked (WI)	Int: Banked (TX)
Financial Education	0.112*	0.249***	-0.0111	0.227**	0.291**	0.195**
	(0.022)	(0.000)	(0.901)	(0.002)	(0.002)	(0.003)
Bank and Education			0.202*	0.0499		
			(0.045)	(0.581)		
Education & Student Banked					-0.266**	0.135
					(0.006)	(0.189)
Observations	660	681	660	681	656	681

Persistence of Treatment Effects

The treatment effect reported in the tables above are captured in surveys taken within several weeks before and after the financial education was delivered. However, we are ultimately interested in the lasting effects of financial education. To assess the persistence of the knowledge gained, 272 5th graders from Eau Claire who participated in the study in the spring of 2012 completed the survey for a third time in the spring of 2013. At this point all participants had financial education, thus the label control refers to students who received it between the first and second follow- up, and treatment refers to those who received it between baseline and the first follow- up. Table 19 (below) shows mean outcomes at each point for each group.

The results of the follow- up are remarkably positive. Each metric improves between baseline and follow- up, and stays at elevated levels a year later. The control group largely catches up after exposure to education. Figure 9 shows the same results as the above table for the treatment group graphically. Each outcome is reported as a ratio of its baseline value. Overall, this is encouraging evidence of effect persistence.

Table 19. Eau Claire Second Year Student Assessment Surveys over Time

	Control			Treatment		
	Baseline	First Follow-up	Second Follow-up	Baseline	First Follow-up	Second Follow-up
Quiz Score (13pt)	6.18	6.58	7.54	5.65	7.93	7.88
Student banked	0.65	0.70	0.74	0.69	0.80	0.78
Spend money immediately (5pt)	2.69	2.49	2.55	2.55	2.24	2.35
Easy to save (5pt)	3.68	3.70	3.66	3.66	3.85	3.88
Saving is for adults (5pt)	1.63	1.46	1.46	1.59	1.39	1.39
Banks useful to you (pt)	3.88	3.93	3.92	3.76	4.11	4.13

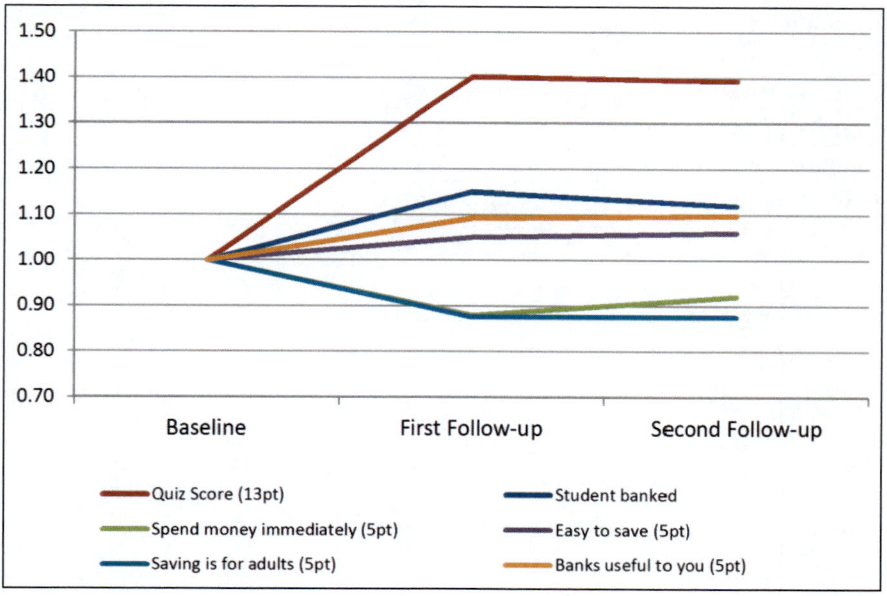

Figure 8. Changes in Outcomes for the Eau Claire Second Year Treatment Group.

Account usage data from the 120 students are presented below as monthly means calculated over the 5.5 months immediately preceding financial education for the treatment group, the 2.5 months immediately after the financial education for the treatment group, and the 7 months starting 7 months after the financial education for the treatment group. This is a small subset of students, but changes in account activity following financial education for the treatment group do not show the same persistence as that of the survey measures.

Table 20. Eau Claire Second Year Sample Average Account Usage over Time

	Control			Treatment		
	Before	Immediately After	Long After	Before	Immediately After	Long After
Number of Deposits	1.20	1.01	1.01	0.96	0.88	0.88
Number of Withdrawals	0.13	0.20	0.15	0.06	0.07	0.13
Gross Deposits	14.43	21.42	15.65	18.11	15.00	18.81
Gross Withdrawals	12.86	22.59	10.26	7.81	6.50	9.05
Number of Transactions	1.33	1.21	1.01	1.02	0.95	1.02
Net Deposits	5.96	1.67	6.47	2.95	12.67	3.23

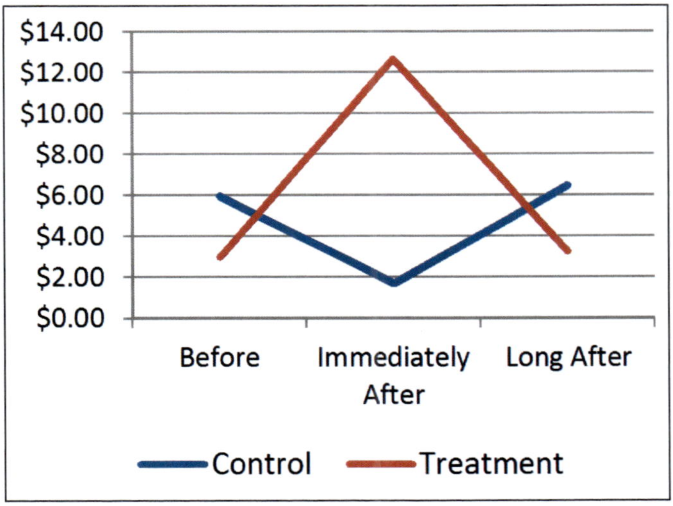

Figure 9. Eau Claire Second Year Sample Average Net Deposits.

Figure 10 displays one of the more striking examples. The students who received the education showed a large increase in net deposits, only to return to pre- education levels close to the control group. These results suggest that the education may have some immediate influence but that saving large amounts was not sustained over time. This is in part driven by unusual withdrawal levels by the control group during the intermediate follow- up period.

It is also clear from the first year bank data that there is considerable variability in deposits both across students and within students over time. Large deposits and withdrawals strongly influence the mean results, and most students do not use their account in a given week. As a result, even the large increase in deposits shown by the treatment group in the first year is not statistically significant.

Summary of Findings

Financial education and the presence of in-school, on- site financial services are associated with:

- **Knowledge Gains**: There are statistically significant positive changes in assessment test scores comparing before and after the education relative to a control group that was randomized by classroom. Students appeared to have learned the material in the courses offered.
- **Additional Knowledge among Banked Students**: Students with bank accounts show stronger effects in term of changes in learning.
- **Banking Access**: Based on school- based variation in access to in-school banking, it appears the likelihood of a student having a bank account was highly correlated with the presence of in-school financial services.
- **Banking Behavior**: Data on student bank accounts suggest that the education is related to students more actively using accounts, although the sub- sample of students with account data was somewhat limited.
- **Improved Attitudes about Savings and Banks**: Attitudes towards saving and financial institutions also improved, with strongest effects from financial education.
- **Persistence of Effects**: Second year follow- up data with one group of students suggests that effects on learning persisted over time.

Table 21. Education and Bank Effect Size

		Financial Education		Bank in School[15]	
Outcome		Effect (sigma units)	Significance	Effect (sigma units)	Significance
Quiz Score (13pt)		0.76	***	-0.01	
Banked (per survey)		0.07	*	0.25	***
Easy to Save (5pt)		0.09	*	0.09	*
Banks Useful to You (5pt)		0.16	***	0.10	**
WI	**Deposits**	0.06		0.01	
	Active Accts	0.01		0.77	*
TX	**Deposits**	-0.16	*	0.09	
	Active Accts	0.19		-0.17	

Table 21 summarizes the average treatment effects of the financial education and the bank in school access overall in standard deviation units. The effects of education are quite large by most standards. The effect sizes for the attitudinal measures in the survey are more modest but still positive.

Estimates using bank behavior to estimate actual banking activity are not as conclusive, in large part due to the smaller sample of students with banking data and a high degree of variation in the data. Using the Amarillo data with randomized in school bank branches and a lottery to offer a $25 seed deposit for student accounts, the effects of banking access can be estimated, in addition to education effects. The main effect of these efforts is to increase the rate at which students have bank accounts and at which students actively use accounts.

IMPLICATIONS FOR POLICY AND RESEARCH

This study offers some of the first rigorous findings on school- based financial education and in-school financial access. These findings are coming at a time of increased interest in financial education and children's savings accounts and thus offer a number of insights for this rapidly expanding field. They also raise important questions about both the role of public policy in encouraging activity, and the role of future research in shedding additional light on the specific facilitators and barriers to saving and financial capability among children, and to implementing such programming efficiently and effectively.

Insight #1: Classroom-Based Financial Education Provides Benefits

Financial education in schools, even small amounts, does appear to increase financial knowledge and capability. The results of this study showed statistically significant positive changes in assessment test scores before and after the education relative to a control group that was randomized by classroom—an increase in the number of correct questions between 1.8 and 2.0. These gains in knowledge were also found to persist a year after receiving the financial education. The education was also linked to small increases in rates of students being banked and to improved student attitudes towards savings and the usefulness of financial institutions.

These are encouraging findings for proponents of classroom- based financial education. Positive results were found after integrating five or six short lessons into classroom instruction, which suggests that financial education need not be tremendously onerous to deliver in order to be effective. However, even "light touch" financial education offerings require commitment and investment on the part of schools and school districts. Indeed, training and support for teachers—and the political will necessary to secure this support—was critical to the success of this pilot. In addition to training on the financial education lessons and lesson plans and classroom materials, teachers participating in this pilot also had the option to attend financial education lessons themselves so that they would feel comfortable teaching the concepts to students. The implication, then, is that to replicate these results, schools and school districts would need to be willing (and/or encouraged) to invest in materials and in-service training for teachers. They might also need guidance in selecting and implementing such materials and training from among the wide array of financial education curricula that exist.

Insight #2: Bank Accounts Facilitate Financial Capability; In-School Banking Facilitates Getting Banked

This study also provides evidence that students do learn more when given an opportunity to apply their learning. Students with bank accounts demonstrated greater knowledge gains compared to students receiving financial education alone, As one teacher in Amarillo observed, students with bank accounts seemed to be generally more engaged in the lessons, as the account made what they were learning relevant. However, having an account was not randomly assigned, so students with such accounts may be different that students without the accounts.

Moreover, having a bank in school may be an effective way to introduce young people to banking and facilitate getting children into accounts. In this study, the likelihood of a student having a bank account was highly correlated with the presence of an in-school bank or credit union branch. While there was not evidence that a branch in school had a direct impact on financial knowledge, in-school access was related to students more actively using their accounts and increases in students' perceptions of ease of saving and whether they consider banks or credit unions to be useful. Increasing the number of partnerships between local banks and credit unions and school districts is a promising strategy for increasing the financial capability of students, particularly when in-school banking programs can be combined with financial education curriculum.

A benefit of working in schools with higher rates of economically disadvantaged students is that in school bank branches may potentially facilitate getting unbanked parents to open checking and savings accounts. The experience of opening a savings account for a child through their local school may make parents who themselves are unbanked more comfortable with financial institutions and more likely to open an account. Through the pilot in Amarillo, we heard anecdotally that parents, and particularly recent immigrants, have a high level of trust in their children's schools and look to their schools for a variety of information and connections to community resources. This appears to align with the experiences of other school- based savings programs that were not part of this study.

However, despite the clear benefits of in-school banks, barriers to expanding their reach do exist. Anecdotal experience from designing other savings program efforts is that not every financial institution is willing to launch in-school banks, and not every school/school district is comfortable with the concept of on- site banking. A primary concern appears to be one of security, risk and liability; some schools, for instance, express worry that on "bank days," children carrying money to school to deposit might be vulnerable to being targeted or bullied, or that the school might face undue liability if they are holding cash for later bank deposit. Similarly, some financial institutions have indicated concern about the risk of taking on- site deposits—specifically, the ability to issue receipts, the carrying of cash back and forth to a branch, etc. Additional outreach and guidance to both schools and financial institutions on these issues, as well as wider distribution generally of information on launching a successful bank- at- school program, would likely prove valuable in encouraging further growth of this important sector.

Insight #3: Financial Institutions Could Use Guidance on Federal and State Laws that Apply to the Children's Savings Marketplace

There is a growing need for guidance regarding federal regulatory and other requirements under state laws—and/or a summary of existing rules or other guidance—that banks and credit unions could use in their efforts to design and create financial products for the rapidly- growing field of children's savings. The primary regulatory issue centers around the federal rules under the Bank Secrecy Act, particularly the so- called "know- your-customer" (KYC) requirements and the Customer Identification Program (CIP) rule. In this regard, banks and credit unions have raised question about the kinds of information and documentation (e.g. Social Security numbers or individual tax account number, birth certificates, etc.) that may be required at the time of establishing an account that would satisfy the CIP rule. In large-scale child savings programs in particular, gathering this kind of information for every child can be onerous at best, and is often administratively cost-prohibitive. Requesting identifying information or verification documents also can result in reductions in child participation if parents are unwilling or unable to produce the required documents.

In this vein, in the Amarillo pilot, the account opening process was complicated by parents' immigration status and the documentation HSB required to open accounts, resulting in the decision to offer two different types of accounts to participating families: joint accounts or child- only accounts. Opening child- only accounts was a feasible solution in this pilot because the accounts are standard savings accounts intended for use by children for making small transactions.

While this issue was solved for the Amarillo pilot, important implications remain for other child savings programs, particularly those conducted on a larger scale. The majority of children's savings initiatives are designed to encourage a meaningful amount of savings for a designated purpose, typically post- secondary education. One approach has been to use an account structure is to open custodial escrow accounts that are owned by an identified third party (e.g., a city or county, a not for- profit entity, etc.), with sub accounts for each individual child. The question for financial institutions is, under the CIP rule and KYC requirements imposed by regulatory agencies and this scenario of custodial accounts, whether banks must require SSNs/ITINs for each child whose name is listed on such a sub- account. The logic for not requiring individual SSNs/ITINs is that the technical "customer" in such an account is not the child, but rather the custodial owner of the account, which, especially if a public or nonprofit agency, is a known entity with a tax ID number.

Some financial institutions have identified ways to establish savings accounts designed for the benefit of minors that adhere to federal regulations and the banks' own internal protocols, but these financial institutions are not publicly sharing the details of the legal/structural process that has allowed them to establish these accounts in accordance with federal and state laws. In the meantime, other financial institutions which are eager to enter the children's savings marketplace are running up against barriers, perceived or real, that are significantly hindering their ability to do so, and in turn, are creating major challenges for emerging child savings initiatives that are struggling to find financial institution partners. Clearly, financial institutions would be served by having a deeper and clearer understanding of what is possible and permissible in this marketplace. Additional written guidance from regulators would go a long way toward removing these (real and/or perceived) barriers, and to opening up the child savings marketplace in the private sector.

Insight #4: Even a Modest Incentive Can Boost Account Take-Up

The $25 seed deposit offered randomly to students in Amarillo led to an 18% increase in students with bank accounts. Savings initiatives interested in offering an incentive or a match frequently question what incentive is the right incentive and what amount is the right amount. Initiatives whose programs don't have account withdrawal restrictions are also interested in whether the seed deposit will be withdrawn. We were not able to test different types and amounts of incentives in this study, but the results from Amarillo suggest that even a modest incentive can be effective in encouraging account take- up. The results also suggest that even without a withdrawal restriction, students and their families leave the seed deposit in their accounts.

Call for Future Research

This study provides strong evidence of the effectiveness of classroom-based financial education and financial access in elementary schools. Future research should examine long- term outcomes associated with these interventions as well as test strategies for increasing their impact. In this section we provide suggestions for how researchers might assist in both these areas.[16]

First, testing different approaches to financial education would help the field better understand how to effectively disseminate financial knowledge and encourage good financial habit formation. There is a range of financial education curricula available; their effectiveness should be tested and compared. Researchers should also attempt to determine the financial education 'dosage' that provides the greatest return on investment. In addition, research into the best age for learning different types of financial knowledge and behavior would be helpful. As more states incorporate financial capability measures into their education testing standards, opportunities to explore these research questions with data from large, diverse samples of students will likely increase.

Second, researchers should explore how to make financial access most effective. Relatively little is known about how much savings incentives matter, what the right kind is and when the right time is to offer them. Randomized controlled trial research that explores how to optimize incentives would help bank- in-school and other children's savings programs better allocate their resources. In addition, research that investigates whether a certain amount in a child's account is necessary to trigger the 'asset effect' or if simply the act of saving is enough to produce this effect would help practitioners set up more effective savings account programs.

Third, more needs to be understood about the long- term effects of financial education and financial access. For this to be possible, high- quality, longitudinal data need to be collected. Longitudinal data would allow researchers to assess the degree to which financial education and financial access effects persist over time. In addition, longitudinal data could be used to explore if financial education and financial product access lead to improved college attendance and lower student debt. Currently, most state departments of education collect detailed longitudinal data on students in local public school districts. These data could potentially be merged with financial education and account access information and with national college enrollment databases to explore long- term financial education outcomes.

The AFCO project also offers methodological lessons for future financial education and access research projects in schools. A large sample of students is necessary to better control for school and teacher effects, and given the patterns of account use observed in this study, an ideal sample would be closer to 2,500 to 3,000 students. Parental involvement was the biggest challenge to our sample size. Parental consent is necessary for human subject protection, but despite, repeated mailings, using PTA and other school newsletters, local media and even calls directly to parents through the district's automated system, the parent consent rate was between 30% and 40% in both communities. Using innovative methods to get parents' consent, such as finding opportunities at school functions to obtain consent in person or getting consent online, may improve response rates. Because of concerns about consent rates, we did not collect data from parents as a part of this study, but doing so would allow you to collect information on student demographics and academic performance as well as parent financial attitudes and behaviors. This additional data would provide useful controls but may also help identify if there are types of student for which the financial education or financial access makes more of a difference.

If rolling out new in-school banking programs, as we did in Amarillo, providing students with more exposure to the program prior to the delivery of the treatment of financial education may also be useful. To meet the timelines of this project, HSB and Amarillo ISD were able to implement both the financial education and roll out the new Kids' Banks within one semester after only a few months of planning. However, timing the launch of the new in-school banks to the beginning of the school year may have not only provided students with more time to participate in the program, but may have been an ideal time to reach parents. We were also not able to conduct a formal process evaluation of the pilots' implementation, and this type of documentation of best practices, particularly around the banking in schools for which there is a dearth of information, is needed to help facilitate successful partnerships between schools and financial institutions on these types of youth savings initiatives.

APPENDIX A. FULL SUMMARY TABLES

	Means						Standard Deviations						Counts		
	Baseline			Follow-up			Baseline			Follow-up					
	Total	Control	Treatment	Total	Control	Treatment	Total	Control	Treatment	Total	Control	Treatment	Total	Control	Treatment
Student banked	52%	52%	53%	59%	57%	60%	50%	50%	50%	49%	50%	49%	1359	584	775
Student savings (6pt)	4.1	4.2	4.1	4.2	4.3	4.2	1.8	1.7	1.8	1.7	1.7	1.8	578	240	338
Bank in school	44%	45%	43%	49%	52%	46%	50%	50%	50%	50%	50%	50%	1343	578	765
Student uses bank in school	38%	37%	39%	41%	40%	41%	49%	48%	49%	49%	49%	49%	639	291	348
Saving for future/college	83%	81%	85%	87%	87%	87%	38%	40%	36%	34%	33%	34%	967	431	536
Earn allowance	57%	59%	56%	62%	61%	62%	50%	49%	50%	49%	49%	49%	1358	584	774
Allowance ($)	11.5	11.9	11.2	9.8	10.2	9.5	36.6	25.4	43.5	11.5	13.3	9.8	646	283	363
Do odd jobs	69%	70%	68%	73%	73%	73%	46%	46%	47%	44%	44%	45%	1344	577	767
Have paid job	19%	18%	20%	23%	22%	25%	39%	38%	40%	42%	41%	43%	1465	639	826

(Continued)

	Means						Standard Deviations						Counts		
	Baseline			Follow-up			Baseline			Follow-up					
	Total	Control	Treatment	Total	Control	Treatment	Total	Control	Treatment	Total	Control	Treatment	Total	Control	Treatment
Q1 Correct	23%	24%	22%	30%	22%	35%	42%	43%	42%	46%	42%	48%	1403	605	798
Q2 Correct	27%	25%	29%	57%	30%	78%	44%	43%	45%	50%	46%	42%	1403	605	798
Q3 Correct	20%	22%	17%	45%	29%	56%	40%	42%	38%	50%	45%	50%	1403	605	798
Q4 Correct	55%	54%	56%	65%	59%	70%	50%	50%	50%	48%	49%	46%	1403	605	798
Q5 Correct	56%	58%	54%	59%	57%	61%	50%	49%	50%	49%	50%	49%	1403	605	798
Q6 Correct	55%	54%	55%	64%	54%	72%	50%	50%	50%	48%	50%	45%	1403	605	798
Q7 Correct	62%	62%	61%	71%	65%	74%	49%	49%	49%	46%	48%	44%	1403	605	798
Q8 Correct	50%	52%	49%	58%	57%	58%	50%	50%	50%	50%	50%	49%	1403	605	798
Q9 Correct	60%	64%	57%	68%	68%	67%	49%	48%	49%	47%	46%	47%	1403	605	798
Q10 Correct	40%	42%	39%	52%	46%	56%	49%	49%	49%	50%	50%	50%	1403	605	798
Q11 Correct	61%	59%	62%	64%	60%	68%	49%	49%	48%	48%	49%	47%	1403	605	798
Q12 Correct	51%	52%	50%	64%	53%	73%	50%	50%	50%	48%	50%	44%	1403	605	798
Q13 Correct	29%	28%	29%	31%	29%	32%	45%	45%	45%	46%	45%	47%	1403	605	798
Quiz score	5.9	5.9	5.8	7.3	6.3	8.0	2.3	2.3	2.4	2.7	2.5	2.6	1403	605	798

	Means						Standard Deviations						Counts		
	Baseline			Follow-up			Baseline			Follow-up					
	Total	Control	Treatment	Total	Control	Treatment	Total	Control	Treatment	Total	Control	Treatment	Total	Control	Treatment
Spend money immediately (5pt)	2.8	2.8	2.8	2.6	2.6	2.6	1.2	1.1	1.2	1.2	1.2	1.2	1345	576	769
Easy to save (5pt)	3.6	3.6	3.6	3.7	3.7	3.8	1.1	1.1	1.1	1.1	1.1	1.1	1349	581	768
Saving is good (5pt)	4.5	4.5	4.5	4.6	4.6	4.6	0.8	0.7	0.8	0.7	0.7	0.7	1345	579	766
Saving is for adults (5pt)	1.8	1.8	1.8	1.6	1.6	1.6	1.1	1.1	1.1	0.9	1.0	0.9	1372	587	785
Kids don't save: parents buy (5pt)	2.1	2.0	2.1	2.0	1.9	2.0	1.0	1.0	1.1	1.0	1.0	1.0	1369	588	781
Kids don't save: parents give $ (5pt)	2.0	2.0	2.0	1.9	1.9	1.9	1.0	1.0	1.1	1.0	1.0	1.0	1370	589	781
Want college (5pt)	4.4	4.4	4.4	4.5	4.6	4.5	1.0	1.0	1.0	0.9	0.8	0.9	1367	587	780

(Continued)

	Means						Standard Deviations						Counts		
	Baseline			Follow-up			Baseline			Follow-up					
	Total	Control	Treatment	Total	Control	Treatment	Total	Control	Treatment	Total	Control	Treatment	Total	Control	Treatment
Expect college (5pt)	4.2	4.2	4.2	4.2	4.3	4.2	0.9	0.9	1.0	1.0	1.0	1.0	1366	586	780
Want to do well in school (5pt)	4.8	4.8	4.8	4.8	4.8	4.8	0.5	0.5	0.6	0.6	0.6	0.5	1366	586	780
Pay attention in class (5pt)	4.2	4.3	4.2	4.2	4.3	4.2	0.8	0.8	0.8	0.8	0.7	0.8	1367	588	779
Take school seriously (5pt)	4.4	4.4	4.3	4.4	4.4	4.4	0.8	0.8	0.8	0.8	0.8	0.8	1367	587	780
Banks useful to you (5pt)	3.9	4.0	3.8	4.0	4.0	4.1	1.1	1.0	1.2	1.1	1.1	1.0	1341	578	763
Banks are for adults (5pt)	2.0	2.0	2.0	1.8	1.8	1.8	1.2	1.1	1.2	1.1	1.1	1.1	1371	590	781
Banks keep $ safe (5pt)	4.0	4.1	4.0	4.2	4.1	4.4	1.0	1.0	1.0	1.0	1.0	1.0	1339	578	761

	Means						Standard Deviations						Counts		
	Baseline			Follow-up			Baseline			Follow-up					
	Total	Control	Treatment	Total	Control	Treatment	Total	Control	Treatment	Total	Control	Treatment	Total	Control	Treatment
Enjoy taking risks (7pt)	4.1	4.2	4.0	4.1	4.1	4.1	1.8	1.8	1.8	1.9	1.9	1.9	1342	578	764
Accept even bet w/3:1 payout	33%	35%	32%	32%	32%	31%	36%	36%	35%	36%	35%	37%	1337	576	761
Accept even bet w/1.5:1 payout	42%	42%	41%	43%	45%	41%	39%	41%	38%	39%	39%	40%	1343	578	765

APPENDIX B. COMPARISONS OF STUDY COMMUNITIES

	Amarillo	Eau Claire
Community Statistics		
Population, 2010	190,695	65,883
White a one, 2010 (a)	77.0%	91.4%
Hispanic or Latino, 2010 (b)	28.8%	1.9%
Language other than English spoken at home, 2007-2011	22.9%	6.6%
Bachelor's degree or higher, of persons age 25+, 2007-2011	22.3%	33.4%
Median household income, 2007-2011	$44,769	$42,226
Persons below poverty level, percent, 2007-2011	16.9%	18.8%
Unbanked Households, 2009*	10.3%	5.4%
School District Statistics, 2011-2012**		
Economically Disadvantaged Students	66.8%	41.0%
White students	38%	81.2%
African American students	10%	2.5%
Hispanic students	44%	3.2%

(a) Includes persons reporting only one race.

(b) Hispanics may be of any race, so also are included in applicable race categories. Source: US Census Bureau State & County QuickFacts.

* Source: CFED estimates derived from a model based on the 2009 FDIC Survey and the 2005-2009 American Community Survey (ACS).

** Source: Texas Education Agency, Performance Reporting and Wisconsin Department of Public Instruction, Wisconsin's Information Network for Successful Schools.

APPENDIX C. SAVINGS ACCOUNT TERMS

Royal Credit Union School $ense Accounts

Description of Account: This is the primary credit union "Savings" Account. You must fill out a membership card and maintain a $5.00 balance in a primary share account for membership in the credit union, allowing you to vote at the annual meeting, if all voting requirements are met, and to obtain other credit union benefits and services. Secondary Savings can be established to meet the Member's needs for separate Savings Accounts. This includes Real Estate Escrow accounts. The Escrow accounts have restrictions for withdrawals for other than tax or insurance purposes. (They all receive the same dividend rate and Annual Percentage Yield.)

Dividends Compounded: Monthly

Dividends Credited: Monthly

Minimu Opening Balance: $5.00 for Primary Savings* and $0.00 for any other Secondary Savings

Minimu Monthly Balance: $5.00 for Primary Savings and $0.00 for any other Secondary Savings

Balance Computation Method: Daily

Account Limitations: Account Transaction Limitations Apply[17]

Charges: See "Special Service Charges" Disclosure[18]

Source: http://www. cu.org/

* Note: For School $ense accounts, Royal Credit Union provides the minimum opening balance of $5.00. The account must be opened jointly with a parent online or at a local branch.

Happy State Bank Kids' Bank Questions and Answers

Q: Is this a "real" savings account?

A: Yes. Your child will be assigned an account number when the account is opened at Happy State Bank.

Q: Is there a charge for the Account?

A: No. Savings accounts will not have a service charge unless the student exceeds the withdrawal limitations of four per quarter. Each excessive withdrawal is then $2.00.

Q: Is there a minimum balance?

A: No. Minors can open an account with any amount and do not have to maintain a minimum balance.

Q: Does this savings account earn interest?

A: Yes.

Q: When is the interest paid on the savings account?

A: The interest is accrued on a daily basis, compounded and paid quarterly.

Q: Who can make deposits?

A: The parent(s) or child can make a deposit i to the account. We cannot accept parents payroll checks, insurance checks, tax refunds or anything of this nature.

Q: Who can make a withdrawal?

A: Any signer on the account can make a withdrawal at any time.

Q: Where can deposits be made?

A: Deposits can be made at the school when the savings bank is open or at any Happy State Bank location.

Q: Where can the withdrawals be made?

A: The withdrawals can be made only at a Happy State Bank location.

Q: How many accounts can my child have?

A: One per child.

Q: Who will accept the money at the School Kids' Bank?

A: Happy State Bank will train students to be tellers and will be supervised by a parent volunteer and a Happy State Bank employee.

Q: Who can I call if I want to know my account balance or have questions about this account?

A: There are several places that you can get information on the account:

a. Any Happy State Bank branch

b. Happ-eBank Online Banking at www.happybank.com

c. Express Line (806) 359- 7737 or toll free (866) 359- 7737

Your child's account can be structured in one of two ways:

Joint Account: child with parent or responsible party provided the following information can be provided.

Note: Both the child and the adult listed on the account have equal rights and obligations to the account, including the ability to deposit, withdrawal and make balance inquires.

Child	Adult
Legal Name	Legal Name
Valid Social Security Number	Valid Social Security Number
Date of Birth	Date of Birth
Physical & Mailing Address	Physical & Mailing Address
	Valid Photo Identification:

Driver's License
State ID Card
Passport with Valid Visa
Green Card
Permanent Resident Card

If the required information listed above cannot be provided then the account can be opened in the child's name alone.

Single–Child Only Account: child as the only owner provided the following information can be provided.

Note: The child is the only owner of the account, therefor, he or she is the only person with rights to the account including the ability to deposit, withdrawal and make balance inquires.

Child
Legal Name
Valid Social Security Number
Date of Birth
Physical & Mailing Address

APPENDIX D. LESSON LEARNING OBJECTIVES

Lesson 1. The Grasshopper and the Ant

At the end of this lesson, the student will be able to:

- Define opportunity cost and interest.
- Analyze the trade- offs and opportunity cost in a decision about saving.
- Identify reasons to save.
- Explain how savings can be used to satisfy future wants.
- Use the concept of opportunity cost to compare the advantages and disadvantages of saving, and to make informed decisions about saving.

- Explain how interest serves as an incentive to save.

Lessons 2-4. Saving Starts with Wanting More

At the end of this lesson, the student will be able to:

- Define savings, economic want, incentive, short- term goals, long-term goals, and interest.
- Explain the elements of a savings plan.
- Give examples of short- term and long term goals.
- Give examples of incentives.
- Compare the advantages and disadvantages of various savings options.

Lesson 5. Managing Money

At the end of this lesson, the student will be able to:

- Define income, expenses, savings, costs, and benefits.
- Explain that because of limited income, people must make choices.
- Analyze the costs and benefits of alternatives.
- Explain how a budget can help people manage income and expenses.

APPENDIX E. TEACHER INSTRUCTIONS FOR LESSON DELIVERY

Money F-I-T

Instructions for Lesson Delivery

Thanks for your help in ensuring that the *Money F- I- T* lessons are successfully delivered to Eau Claire's 4th and 5th graders! Teachers should review the information below and contact Nicole Truog at the C nter for

Financial Security with any questions. She can be reached at (608) 262- 6766 or ntruog@wisc.edu.

Money F-I-T timeline

The *Money F- I- T* schedule differs depending on whether you have a Group A or Group B classroom. The group list is appended at the end of this document. Teachers should do their best to deliver lessons according to the schedule, but please contact Nicole Truog if you need to make adjustments.

Before any *Money - I- T* lessons are taught, all teachers should administer the first student questionnaire to their students between **March 13** and **March 15**. It is very important to the success of the *Money F- I- T* evaluation that **Group A** lessons are delivered between the first and second questionnaires, and **Group B** lessons are delivered after the second questionnaire. Please review the draft instructions for administering the questionnaires. Final instructions will be provided when the questionnaires are delivered to your school.

If you did not attend the training, a Royal Credit Union staff member will contact you about scheduling times to teach the lessons in your classroom. Please contact us if you have not heard from RCU by **March 15**.

Group A

March 12	Student questionnaires delivered to partnership coordinators
March 13 March 15	1st student questionnaire administered by teachers
March 16	Completed student questionnaires collected from partnership coordinators
Week of March 19	Spring Break
Week of March 26	*Money F-I-T* Lesson 1 delivered in classrooms
Week of April 2	*Money F-I-T* Lesson 2 delivered in classrooms
Week of April 9	*Money F-I-T* Lesson 3 delivered in classrooms
Week of April 16	*Money F-I-T* Lesson 4 delivered in classrooms
Week of April 23	*Money F-I-T* Lesson 5 delivered in classrooms

Week of April 30	2nd student questionnaire administered by teachers (specific dates that week will be determined in April)

Group B

March 12	Student questionnaires delivered to partnership coordinators
March 13 March 15	1st student questionnaire administered by teachers
March 16	Completed student questionnaires collected from partnership coordinators
Week of March 19	Spring Break
Week of April 30	2nd student questionnaire administered by teachers (specific dates that week will be determined in April)
Week of May 7 to the end of the year	*Money F-I-T* lessons delivered in classrooms according to schedule determined by teachers and RCU educators (lessons may begin as soon as the 2nd questionnaire has been administered)

Teacher Feedback

Within **3 days** of the delivery of each lesson, we would like you to visit the *Money F-I-T* website to complete a survey to provide feedback about the lessons. The survey will be available under the Teachers tab (http://moneyfitcfs.wordpress.com/teachers/). Teachers who respond to the survey after all 5 lessons will receive $25 for their time. We would like all teachers to complete the surveys (whether the lessons were taught by a teacher or RCU educator). If you are having an RCU educator deliver the lessons, please be present in the classroom while lessons are taught so you can provide feedback.

Lesson delivery: Additional information

All lesson materials will be posted on the school district's P- drive in the *Money F I- T* folder. Please contact Kris Dimock with any questions about accessing this information. If you would like additional copies of student worksheets or other curriculum materials, please contact Nicole Truog.

OpportunityTexas™

LEARN. EARN. SAVE.

Smarter Texans Save

Instructions for Lesson Delivery

Thanks for your help in ensuring that the *Smarter Texans Save* lessons are successfully delivered at the appropriate time to Amarillo 4th graders! Teachers should review the information below and contact Laura Rosen, OpportunityTexas Coordinator, with any questions. She can be reached at (512) 823 2868 or rosen@cppp.org.

If you would like additional copies of stud nt worksheets or other curriculum materials, please contact Cindy Manzano, Smarter Texas Director at the Texas Council on Economic Education, at cindy@economicstexas.org and by phone at 713- 503- 5338.

Smarter Texans Save Timeline

The *Smarter Texans Save* lesson delivery schedule, listed on the back side of this sheet, differs depending on whether you are a Group A or Group B teacher. The group list is appended at the end of this document. Teachers should do their best to deliver lessons according to the schedule, but please contact Laura Rosen if you need to make adjustments.

Before any Smarter Texans Save lessons are taught, all teachers (both Group A and Group B teachers) need to administer the student pre - survey to their students between ***February 1 and February 6****. It is very important to the success of the Smarter Texans Save evaluation that* ***Group A's*** *lessons are delivered* ***between*** *the pre and second/post assessment surveys, and* ***Group B's*** *lessons are delivered* ***after*** *the second/post survey.*

Because of an unforeseen delay in study approval, we had to push back the pre- survey delivery date by nearly a week for all teachers and the lesson delivery timeline for **Group A** teachers by a week. Because of this, **Group A** teachers will need to teach two lessons the week of February 18, noted on the timeline on the back of this page. We apologize for the slight compression of the lesson delivery timeline for **Group A** teachers.

Group A Timeline

February 1	Student assessment pre- surveys delivered to assistant principals/school study contact
Feb. 1- 6	Student assessment pre- survey administered by teachers ***before*** Lesson 1 is delivered
Week of Feb. 4	*Smarter Texans Save* Lesson 1 delivered in classrooms ***after*** teacher administers assessment pre-survey
Feb. 8	Completed student assessment pre- surveys collected from assistant principals/school study contact
Week of Feb. 11	*Smarter Texans Save* Lesson 2 delivered in classrooms
Week of Feb. 18	*Smarter Texans Save* Lesson 3 delivered in classrooms
Week of Feb. 18	*Smarter Texans Save* Lesson 4 delivered in classrooms
Week of Feb. 25	*Smarter Texans Save* Lesson 5 delivered in classrooms
Week of March 4	*Smarter Texans Save* Lesson 6 delivered in classrooms
Week of March 4	Second/post- student assessment survey administered by teachers ***after*** Lesson 6 is delivered
Week of March 18	Completed student assessment surveys collected from assistant principals/school study contact

Group B Timeline

February 1	Student assessment pre- surveys delivered to assistant principals/school study contact
Feb. 1- 6	Student assessment pre- survey administered by

	teachers
Feb 8	Completed student assessment pre survey collected from assistant principals/school study contact
Week of March 4	Second/post- student assessment survey administered by teachers
Week of March 18	Completed student assessment surveys collected from assistant principals
After STAAR testing – end of school year	*Smarter Texans Save* lessons delivered in classrooms according to schedule determined by teachers (lessons may begin any time after the second/post assessment survey has been administered ***and*** after STAAR testing)

Teacher Feedback

Within **3 days** of the delivery of each lesson, we would like you to visit the *Smarter Texans Save* website to complete a feedback form to provide feedback about the lessons. The form will be available under the Teachers' tab (http://smartertexanssave.wordpress.com/teachers/). Teachers who respond to the survey after all 6 lessons will receive $90 for their time ($15 for each lesson feedback form completed), which will be given to teachers on a gift card at the end of the spring semester. We would like all teachers to complete the feedback forms (see next page).

Return of Study Consent Forms

The folders you received on Feb. 1 with study materials included envelopes for each student that you were instructed to send home with them the day you conducted the student assessment pre-survey. This envelope includes a letter to parents explaining the study and a study consent form. Students will be returning completed consent forms to school. **When you receive completed consent forms from students, please deposit them in the study Drop Box in the school office.**

Appendix F. Summary of School-Based Financial Education Studies

Authors	Grade Level	Control Group	Students	Measures	Results
Berti and Monaci (1998)	3	Yes	58 (25 T; 33 C)	Pre/post (10 days later and 4 months later)	Knowledge gains (at 4 months)
Diem et al. (2006)	6–8	No	500	Pre/post	Knowledge gains; Attitude gains
Go et al. (2012)	4–5	Yes	403(220 T; 183 C)	Pre/post/ follow-up (3 months post)	Attitude gains Self-reported behavioral changes
Grody et al. (2008)	3	Yes	47 (31 T; 16 C)	10 pre/post multiple choice questions (read aloud)	Knowledge gains
Harter and Harter (2009)	3–12	Yes	699–995 (varies)	Pre/post	Knowledge gains
Schug and Hagedorn (2005)	2–3	No	316	10 pre/post (read aloud)	Knowledge gains (7 of 10 items)
Sherraden et al. (2011)	K–4	No	200	Post only (4th-grade survey)	Knowledge gains; No saving gains
Smith, Sharp, and Campbell (2011)	6–8	No	160	Pre/post	Knowledge gains; No attitude or confidence gains
Sosin, Dick, and Reiser (1997)	3–6	Yes	382(150 T; 232 C)	Pre/post	Knowledge gains

APPENDIX G. STUDENT ASSESSMENTS

1) Eau Claire *Money F-I-T* student assessment
2) Amarillo *Smarter Texans Save* student assessment

OMB Control #1505-0242

Center for Financial Security

UNIVERSITY OF WISCONSIN-MADISON

Eau Claire *Money F-I-T* Survey

Label applied here with student name, ID number Teacher and School Name

1. Do you currently have a savings account at a bank or credit union in your own name?

○ Yes
○ No → **Go to Question 3**
○ Don't know or not sure

2. If you have a savings account, about how much money do you think is currently in the account?

○ $1 to $25
○ $26 to $50
○ $51 to $100
○ $101 to $200
○ $201 to $500
○ More than $500
○ Don't know or not sure

3. Does your school let kids with savings accounts put money in the accounts at school?

○ Yes
○ No → **Go to Question 5**
○ Don't know or not sure

4. If yes, do you put money in a savings account while you are at school?

○ Yes
○ No
○ Don't know or not sure

5. Are you saving money for future schooling, like college?

○ Yes
○ No
○ Don't know or not sure

6. Do you get pocket money or an allowance?

○ Yes
○ No → **Go to Question 8**
○ Don't know or not sure

7. If yes, how much money do you get per week? [ ]

8. Do you sometimes do small jobs at home, such as washing dishes, to earn money?

○ Yes
○ No
○ Don't know or not sure

9. Do you have a paid job outside of school, such as a paper route or baby-sitting job?

○ Yes
○ No
○ Don't know or not sure

10. The next questions are about money, and some of the words people use when talking about money. Please choose <u>one</u> answer for each question.

Juan put his money in a savings account. The payment that the bank makes to Juan for the use of his money while it is deposited in the bank is called…

○ …interest
○ …wages
○ …credit
○ …profit
○ …don't know or not sure

11. Shawna got $20 for her birthday. She wants to either save her money for a radio, or spend it on a shirt. If she buys the shirt, saving for the radio is her...

O ...expense
O ...revenue
O ...human capital
O ...opportunity cost
O ...don't know or not sure

12. Ming wanted to buy a fancy notebook for school <u>and</u> save her money to buy a computer. Ming decided to buy a plain notebook that is less expensive so she can save more money for the computer. Ming's decision is an example of...

O ...paying interest
O ...depositing money
O ...making a tradeoff
O ...choosing a service
O ...don't know or not sure

13. Duane earned $25 raking leaves. He spent $20 of the $25 on a video game. The $5 that he did not spend is called his...

O ...interest
O ...saving
O ...profit
O ...wage
O ...don't know or not sure

14. Marisa had $50 in her checking account. She made a withdrawal of $10 and a deposit of $20. What is Marisa's balance in her checking account?

O $10
O $20
O $50
O $60
O Don't know or not sure

15. Janis wants to save $75 for a CD player. She plans to save $5 a month. What else does Janis need in her savings plan?

O A checking account
O A certificate of deposit
O The number of stores selling CD players
O The number of months that she must save
O Don't know or not sure

16. Scott plans to save the same amount of money each week for 10 weeks to buy his mom a $30 necklace. How much money should Scott save each week?

O $1
O $2
O $3
O $4
O Don't know or not sure

17. The best example of a long-term goal would be saving for a…

- O …video game
- O …birthday present
- O …college education
- O …pair of basketball shoes
- O …don't know or not sure

18. Sara Wilson earns an income of $3,000 per month as an elementary school teacher. She has expenses of $2,000 each month. The amount she has left over each month is called…

- O …profit
- O …credit
- O …saving
- O …budget
- O …don't know or not sure

19. The Walker family went on a summer vacation in the mountains. They must have decided that the benefits of the vacation were…

- O …greater than the cost
- O …less than the cost
- O …zero
- O …don't know or not sure

20. A plan for managing income, spending and saving is called…

- O …a budget
- O …an investment
- O …a credit account
- O …an account balance
- O …don't know or not sure

21. Which one of the following families is <u>saving</u> money each month?

- O The Smiths have $750 in income, and $800 in expenses
- O The Suiters have $1,500 in income, and $1,500 in expenses
- O The Wilburns have $1,000 in income, and $900 in expenses
- O The Jacksons have $1,200 in income and $1,300 in expenses
- O Don't know or not sure

22. Imagine you open a bank account and deposit $100. The account earns 10 percent interest per year. How much would you have in the account at the end of two years?

- O Exactly $102
- O Exactly $120
- O Less than $120
- O More than $120
- O Don't know or not sure

23. Next we have some questions about how you feel about spending and saving.

How often do you find it hard to avoid spending money immediately, like within 1 or 2 days?

- O Never
- O Almost never
- O Sometimes
- O Most of the time
- O Always

24. How often do you find it easy to save money?

- O Never
- O Almost never
- O Sometimes
- O Most of the time
- O Always

25. Is it good to save money?

- O Not at all
- O A little bit
- O Somewhat
- O Very
- O Extremely

26. Some kids feel that saving money is only for adults. How often to you feel that way?

- O Never
- O Almost never
- O Sometimes
- O Most of the time
- O Always

27. Some kids feel they don't need to save money, because their parents will buy them the things they like. How often to you feel that way?

- O Never
- O Almost never
- O Sometimes
- O Most of the time
- O Always

28. Some kids feel they don't need to save money, because the money their parents give them is for spending. How often to you feel that way?

- O Never
- O Almost never
- O Sometimes
- O Most of the time
- O Always

29. Next we have some questions about how you feel about school and college.

How much do you want to attend college?

○ Not at all
○ A little
○ Somewhat
○ Very much
○ Absolutely

30. Many people do not attend college, even though they want to.

How much do you expect to attend college?

○ Not at all
○ A little
○ Somewhat
○ Very much
○ Absolutely

31. Do you want to do well at school?

○ Not at all
○ A little
○ Somewhat
○ Very much
○ Absolutely

32. Do you pay attention in class?

○ Never
○ Almost never
○ Sometimes
○ Most of the time
○ Absolutely

33. Do you take school seriously?

○ Not at all
○ A little
○ Somewhat
○ Very
○ Extremely

34. Next we have some questions about how you feel about banks.

Do you think banks and credit unions provide services that are useful to you?

○ Not at all
○ Slightly
○ Somewhat
○ Very much
○ Absolutely

35. Some kids feel that bank accounts are only for adults. How often to you feel that way?

- O Never
- O Almost never
- O Sometimes
- O Most of the time
- O Always

36. Do you think banks and credit unions are a safe place for people to keep their money?

- O Not at all
- O Slightly
- O Somewhat
- O Very much
- O Absolutely

37. The last few questions are about how you feel about taking risks.

Some people enjoy taking risks, others avoid them. How about you, do you…

- O …always avoid them?
- O …usually avoid them?
- O …sometimes avoid them?
- O …neither avoid nor enjoy them?
- O …sometimes enjoy them?
- O …usually enjoy them?
- O …always enjoy them?

38. Imagine that you have won $100 in a raffle. When you go to pick up your $100, the person with the money offers to give you $300 instead, if you flip the quarter in your pocket and it comes up heads. If it comes up tails, you get $0. If you don't want to flip the coin, you may take your $100 and leave. Do you agree to flip the coin?

- O No way
- O Maybe
- O Yes

39. Now imagine that you have won $100 in a raffle. When you go to pick up your $100, the person with the money offers to give you $150 instead, if you flip the quarter in your pocket and it comes up heads. If it comes up tails, you get $50. If you don't want to flip the coin, you may take your $100 and leave. Do you agree to flip the coin?

- O No way
- O Maybe
- O Yes

Thank you for completing this survey! Please return it to your teacher now.

OpportunityTexas™

LEARN. EARN. SAVE.

Smarter Texans Save Survey

Label applied here with student name, ID number Teacher and School Name

1. Do you currently have a savings account at a bank or credit union in your own name?

- ○ Yes
- ○ No → **Go to Question 3**
- ○ Don't know or not sure

2. If you have a savings account, about how much money do you think is currently in the account?

- ○ $1 to $25
- ○ $26 to $50
- ○ $51 to $100
- ○ $101 to $200
- ○ $201 to $500
- ○ More than $500
- ○ Don't know or not sure

3. Does your school let kids with savings accounts put money in the accounts at school?

- ○ Yes
- ○ No → **Go to Question 5**
- ○ Don't know or not sure

4. If yes, do <u>you</u> put money in a savings account while you are at school?

- ○ Yes
- ○ No
- ○ Don't know or not sure

5. Are you saving money for future schooling, like college?

- ○ Yes
- ○ No
- ○ Don't know or not sure

6. Do you get pocket money or an allowance?

○ Yes
○ No → **Go to Question 8**
○ Don't know or not sure

7. If yes, how much money do you get per week? ☐

8. Do you sometimes do small jobs at home, such as washing dishes, to earn money?

○ Yes
○ No
○ Don't know or not sure

9. Do you have a paid job outside of school, such as a paper route or baby-sitting job?

○ Yes
○ No
○ Don't know or not sure

10. The next questions are about money, and some of the words people use when talking about money. Please choose one answer for each question.

Juan put his money in a savings account. The payment that the bank makes to Juan for the use of his money while it is deposited in the bank is called…

○ …interest
○ …wages
○ …credit
○ …profit
○ …don't know or not sure

11. Ming wanted to buy a fancy notebook for school and save her money to buy a computer. Ming decided to buy a plain notebook that is less expensive so she can save more money for the computer. Ming's decision is an example of…

○ …paying interest
○ …depositing money
○ …making a tradeoff
○ …choosing a service
○ …don't know or not sure

12. Duane earned $25 raking leaves. He spent $20 of the $25 on a video game. The $5 that he did not spend is called his…

○ …interest
○ …saving
○ …profit
○ …wage
○ …don't know or not sure

13. Marisa had $50 in her checking account. She made a withdrawal of $10 and a deposit of $20. What is Marisa's balance in her checking account?

○ $10
○ $20
○ $50
○ $60
○ Don't know or not sure

14. Janis wants to save $75 for a CD player. She plans to save $5 a month. What else does Janis need in her savings plan?

○ The number of months that she must save
○ The number of stores selling CD players
○ A certificate of deposit
○ A checking account
○ Don't know or not sure

15. Scott plans to save the same amount of money each week for 10 weeks to buy his mom a $30 necklace. How much money should Scott save each week?

○ $1
○ $2
○ $3
○ $4
○ Don't know or not sure

16. Sara Wilson earns an income of $3,000 per month as an elementary school teacher. She has expenses of $2,000 each month. The amount she has left over each month is called...

○ ...profit
○ ...credit
○ ...saving
○ ...budget
○ ...don't know or not sure

17. The Walker family went on a summer vacation in the mountains. They must have decided that the benefits of the vacation were...

○ ...greater than the cost
○ ...less than the cost
○ ...zero
○ ...don't know or not sure

18. A plan for managing income, spending and saving is called...

○ ...a budget
○ ...an investment
○ ...a credit account
○ ...an account balance
○ ...don't know or not sure

19. Which one of the following families is saving money each month?

- ○ The Smiths have $750 in income, and $800 in expenses
- ○ The Suiters have $1,500 in income, and $1,500 in expenses
- ○ The Wilburns have $1,000 in income, and $900 in expenses
- ○ The Jacksons have $1,200 in income and $1,300 in expenses
- ○ Don't know or not sure

20. On Ella's tenth birthday, her grandmother decided to give her $500 to start saving for college. Ella's goal is the keep the money safe while making money.

In order to meet her goal, Ella should…

- ○ … put her money in a piggy bank and hide it in her closet until she is ready to go to college.
- ○ … buy an expensive doll and hope that she can sell it for more when she goes to college.
- ○ … buy everything she wants now and worry about college when she is older.
- ○ … put the money in a savings account at a bank.

21. Which of the following is a fixed expense for a person?

- ○ clothing
- ○ gasoline
- ○ apartment rent
- ○ video rentals

22. Each week, Mason gets a $10 allowance and earns $20 for babysitting. Mason created the table below to help decide how he will spend his money.

Entertainment:	$11.50
Charity:	$3.25
Save for college:	$11.00
Save for skateboard:	

Based on Mason's earnings and the table above, how much will Mason be able to save for the skateboard?

- ○ $4.25
- ○ $4.75
- ○ $5.00
- ○ $5.25

23. Next we have some questions about how you feel about spending and saving.

How often do you find it hard to avoid spending money immediately, like within 1 or 2 days?

- ○ Never
- ○ Almost never
- ○ Sometimes
- ○ Most of the time
- ○ Always

24. How often do you find it easy to save money?

○ Never
○ Almost never
○ Sometimes
○ Most of the time
○ Always

25. Is it good to save money?

○ Not at all
○ A little bit
○ Somewhat
○ Very
○ Extremely

26. Some kids feel that saving money is only for adults. How often to you feel that way?

○ Never
○ Almost never
○ Sometimes
○ Most of the time
○ Always

27. Some kids feel they don't need to save money, because their parents will buy them the things they like. How often to you feel that way?

○ Never
○ Almost never
○ Sometimes
○ Most of the time
○ Always

28. Some kids feel they don't need to save money, because the money their parents give them is for spending. How often to you feel that way?

○ Never
○ Almost never
○ Sometimes
○ Most of the time
○ Always

29. Next we have some questions about how you feel about school and college.

How much do <u>you</u> want to attend college?

○ Not at all
○ A little
○ Somewhat
○ Very much
○ Absolutely

30. Many people do not attend college, even though they want to.

How much do you <u>expect</u> to attend college?

○ Not at all
○ A little
○ Somewhat
○ Very much
○ Absolutely

31. Do you want to do well at school?

○ Not at all
○ A little
○ Somewhat
○ Very much
○ Absolutely

32. How many times have you been to a bank or a credit union with your parents?

○ Never
○ 1-2 times
○ 3-4 times
○ 5 or more times
○ Not sure

33. Do you pay attention in class?

○ Never
○ Almost never
○ Sometimes
○ Most of the time
○ Absolutely

34. Do you take school seriously?

○ Not at all
○ A little
○ Somewhat
○ Very
○ Extremely

35. Next we have some questions about how you feel about banks.

Do you think banks and credit unions provide services that are useful to you?

○ Not at all
○ Slightly
○ Somewhat
○ Very much
○ Absolutely

36. Do you think banks and credit unions are a safe place for people to keep their money?

- ○ Not at all
- ○ Slightly
- ○ Somewhat
- ○ Very much
- ○ Absolutely

37. Some kids feel that bank accounts are only for adults. How often to you feel that way?

- ○ Never
- ○ Almost never
- ○ Sometimes
- ○ Most of the time
- ○ Always

38. The last few questions are about how you feel about taking risks.

Some people enjoy taking risks, others avoid them. How about you, do you…

- ○ …always avoid them?
- ○ …usually avoid them?
- ○ …sometimes avoid them?
- ○ …neither avoid nor enjoy them?
- ○ …sometimes enjoy them?
- ○ …usually enjoy them?
- ○ …always enjoy them?

39. Imagine that you have won $100 in a raffle. When you go to pick up your $100, the person with the money offers to give you $300 instead, if you flip the quarter in your pocket and it comes up heads. If it comes up tails, you get $0. If you don't want to flip the coin, you may take your $100 and leave. Do you agree to flip the coin?

- ○ No way
- ○ Maybe
- ○ Yes

40. Now imagine that you have won $100 in a raffle. When you go to pick up your $100, the person with the money offers to give you $150 instead, if you flip the quarter in your pocket and it comes up heads. If it comes up tails, you get $50. If you don't want to flip the coin, you may take your $100 and leave. Do you agree to flip the coin?

- ○ No way
- ○ Maybe
- ○ Yes

Thank you for completing this survey! Please return it to your teacher now.

REFERENCES

Berti, A. E. & Monaci, M. G. (1998). Third Graders Acquisition of Knowledge of Banking: Restructuring or Accretion?. *British Journal of Educational Psychology*, *68*(3), 357- 371.

Council for Economic Education. (2012). *Survey of the States 2011: the state of economic and personal finance education in our nation's schools*. New York: Council for Economic Education.

Elliott III, W., Choi, E. H., Destin, M. & Kim, K. H. (2011). The Age Old Question, Which Comes First? A Simultaneous Test of Children s Savings and Children s College- bound Identity. *Children & Youth Services Review*, *33*(7), 1101- 1111.

Elliott, W. & Beverly, S. (2011). The role of savings and wealth in reducing 'wilt' between expectations and college attendance. *Journal of Children and Poverty, 17*(2), 165- 185.

Fox, J. & Bartholomae, S. (1999). Student Learning Style and Educational Outcomes: Evidence from a Family Financial Management Course. *Financial Services Review*, *8*(4), 235- 251.

Grinstein-Weiss, M., Spader, J., Yeo, Y., Freeze, E. B. & Taylor, A. (2009). Teach Your Children Well: Credit Outcomes and Prior Parental Teaching of Money Management. Working Paper. Chapel Hill, NC: University of North Carolina at Chapel Hill Center for Community Capital.

Grody, A., Grody, D., Kromann, E. & Sutliff, J. (2008). A Financial Literacy and Financial Services Program for Elementary School Grades- Results of a Pilot Study.

Johnson, E. & Sherraden, M. S. (2007). From Financial Literacy to Financial Capability among Youth. *J. Soc. & Soc. Welfare*, *34*(3), 119- 145.

Kolb, D. A., Boyatzis, R. E. & Mainemelis, C. (2000). Experiential Learning Theory: Previous Research and New Directions. In *Perspectives on Cognitive, Learning, and Thinking Styles*, edited by R. J. Sternberg and L. F. Zhang. NJ: Lawrence Erlbaum, 2000.

Kourilsky M. L. & Carlson, S. R. (1996). Mini- society and YESS! Learning Theory in Action. *Children's Social and Economics Education*, *1*(2).

Lucey, T A. & Giannangelo, D. M. (2006). Short Changed: The Importance of Facilitating Equitable Financial Education in Urban Society. *Education and Urban Society*, *38*(3), 268- 287.

Mandell, L. (2009). The financial literacy of young American adults: Results of the 2008 National ump $ tart Coalition survey of high school seniors and college students." University of Washington and the Aspen Institute.

Mandell, L. & Klein, L. S. (2007). Motivation and Financial Literacy. *Financial Services Review*, *16*(2), 105- 116.

Mandell, L. & Klein, L. S. (2009). The Impact of Financial Literacy Education on Subsequent Financial Behavior. *Journal of Financial Counseling and Planning*, *20*(1), 16- 24.

McCormick, M. H. (2009). The Effectiveness of Youth Financial Education: A Review of the Literature. *Journal of Financial Counseling and Planning*, *20*(1), 71.

Peng, T. C. M., Bartholomae, S., Fox, J. J. & Cravener, G. (2007). The Impact of Personal Finance Education Delivered in High School and College Courses. *Journal of Family and Economic Issues*, *28*(2), 265- 284.

Rand, D. & Slay, K. E. (2008). Using Student- Run Banks to Promote Financial Education and Community Economic and Workforce Development. *Clearinghouse REVIEW Journal of Poverty Law and Policy*, *42*(1/2), 71.

Schug, M. C. & Hagedorn, E. A. (2005). The Money Savvy Pig™ Goes to the Big City: Testing the Effectiveness of an Economics Curriculum for Young Children. *The Social Studies*, *96*(2), 68 71.

Sherraden, M. S., Johnson, L., Guo, B. & Elliott, W. (2011). Financial Capability in Children: Effects of Participation in a School- based Financial Education and Savings Program. *Journal of Family & Economic Issues*, *32*(3), 385- 399.

Sherraden, M. S. (2010). Financial Capability: What is It, and How Can It Be Created. CSD Working Paper 10- 17. St. Louis: Washington University Center for Social Development.

Sherraden, Margaret. S., Johnson, L., Guo, B. & Elliott, W. (2010). Financial capability in children: Effects of participation in a school-based financial education and savings program. *Journal of Family and Economic Issues, 32*(3), 385- 399.

Sosin, K., Dick, J. & Reiser, M. L. (1997). Determinants of Achievement of Economics Concepts by Elementary School Students. *The Journal of Economic Education*, *28*(2), 100 121.

Suiter, M. & Meszaros, B. (2005). Teaching about Saving and Investing in the Elementary and Middle School Grades. *Social Education*, *69*(2), 92- 95.

Valentine, G. & Khayum, M. (2005). Financial Literacy Skills of Students in Urban

Walstad, W. B., K. Rebeck, et al. (2010). The Effects of Financial Education on the Financial Knowledge of High School Students. *Journal of Consumer Affairs*, *44*(2), 336- 357.

Webley, P. (2005). Children's Understanding of Economics. In *Children's Understanding of Society*, edited by M. Barrett and E. Buchanan- Barrow. New York: Psychology Press: 43- 65.

Webley, P. & Nyhus, E. K. (2006). Parents Influence on Children s Future Orientation and Saving. *Journal of Economic Psychology*, *27*(1), 140-164.

End Notes

[1] OpportunityTexas is a joint venture of the Center for Public Policy Priorities and RAISE Texas.

[2] See http://moneyfitcfs.com

[3] For every 500 deposits made at a school site, RCU donates $250 to the school.

[4] In Amarillo, some of the schools have departmental math teachers who teach more than one section of students and, in some schools, up to three or four sections. So that each teacher taught the same lessons at the same time to all of their classes, the financial education in Amarillo was randomized by teacher rather than by classroom as in Eau Claire.

[5] The Texas Council on Economic Education's (TCEE) lessons and the power point that supports each lesson was made available on www.smartertexas.org.

[6] HSB requires a social security number (SSN) to open an account, so if there was not a parent or responsible party with a SSN, the child was able to open an account in his or her name only. Approximately 26% of the accounts opened through this pilot were child- only accounts.

[7] The analysis presented in this report combines the 15 Amarillo schools where the in-school bank branch was created at random with the 3 Amarillo schools where the bank was in existence before the study began. We may expect that the effects of a bank in school differ depending on whether it is newly created and/or whether its presence in the school occurs at random. However, all results presented here are robust to excluding the latter 3 schools.

[8] The $25 incentive was not funded by the U.S. Treasury Department but was provided through private funds raised by OpportunityTexas through the Amarillo Area Community Foundation.

[9] HSB made the new Kids' Banks available to all students in the schools, not just the 4th graders, and a total of 615 new accounts were opened by all students during the study period.

[10] Percentage of economically disadvantaged students during the 2011- 2012 school year calculated by OpportunityTexas based on data from the Texas Education Agency. Economically disadvantaged is defined as students that qualify for free or reduced price lunches.

[11] A small number of transactions above 1,000 dollars are discarded to remove data that are much more likely to represent parental rather than student behavior.

[12] Note that whether or not a student is banked was self- reported by the students, which may be an unreliable measure. In the first year in Eau Claire, we collected data from parents (discontinued in the second year of the pilot to increase the consent rate), and asked about their child's banked status. While the majority of reports agreed, there were inconsistencies between parent and student responses. The most common disagreement involved the parent reporting that the student does have a bank account, while the student said the opposite. This suggests that the student was unaware of their own bank account.

[13] Other checks not shown involved excluding all observations with absolute value of net deposits greater than $250 (median regressions are not feasible because approximately 80% of the observations are 0).

[14] The questions How often do you find it hard to avoid spending money immediately, like within 1 or 2 days? How often do you find it easy to save money?; Some kids feel that saving money is only for adults. How often to you feel that way? used (1) Never (2) Almost never (3) Sometimes (4) Most of the time (5) Always. And then Do you think banks and credit unions provide services that are useful to you? used (1) Not at all (2) Slightly (3) Somewhat (4) Very much (5) Absolutely.

[15] Estimates for bank data in Amarillo reflect effect of seed money rather than bank in school. Virtually all bank data in Amarillo comes from students with a bank in school.

[16] For additional discussion, see Collins, J. Michael and Odders- White, Elizabeth R., (2013). "A Framework for Developing and Testing Financial Capability Programs Targeted to Elementary Schools." Available at SSRN: http://ssrn.com/abstract=2330754

[17] For RCU youth savings accounts, there is no deposit limit. Students may withdraw up to $20 per banking day at their school with a joint member's signature.

[18] Charges refer to additional RCU services above standard use of savings accounts (e.g. duplicate statements or duplicate tax reporting forms). There is a $1.00 service charge for account inquiries handled through RCU Member Service over the phone. There is a $10 charge when more than six transfers, withdrawals, or preauthorized payments are made from a savings account without an account owner's presence at an RCU branch or ATM (Regulation D permits six free transactions).

In: Improving the Financial Capability … ISBN: 978-1-63483-045-4
Editor: Lawrence Rodriguez

Chapter 2

SAVING AND INVESTING FOR STUDENTS*

U.S. Securities and Exchange Commission

DEAR STUDENT

While money doesn't grow on trees, it can grow when you save and invest wisely. Knowing how to secure your financial well-being is one of the most important things you'll ever need in life. You don't have to be a genius to do it. You just need to know a few basics, form a plan, and be ready to stick to it. No matter how much or little money you have, the important thing is to educate yourself about your opportunities. In this brochure, we'll cover the basics on saving and investing.

At the SEC, we enforce the laws that determine how investments are offered and sold to you. These laws protect investors, but you need to do your part, too. Part of this brochure tells you how to check out investments to ensure you do not fall victim to fraud or costly mistakes.

No one can guarantee that you'll make money from investments you make. But if you get the facts about saving and investing and follow through with an intelligent plan, you should be able to gain financial security over the years and enjoy the benefits of managing your money.

* This is an edited, reformatted and augmented version of a publication, SEC Pub. 075, issued by the Office of Investor Education and Advocacy at the U.S. Securities and Exchange Commission.

Please feel free to contact us with any of your questions or concerns about investing. It always pays to learn before you invest. And congratulations on taking your first step on the road to financial security!

U.S. Securities and Exchange Commission
Office of Investor Education and Advocacy
100 F Street, N.E.
Washington, D.C. 20549-0213
Toll-free: (800) SEC-0330
Website: www.investor.gov

DON'T WAIT TO GET STARTED

You Can Do It! It's Easier Than You Think

No one is born knowing how to save or to invest. Every successful investor starts with the basics—the information in this brochure. A few people may stumble into financial security—a wealthy relative may die, or a business may take off. But for most people, the only way to attain financial security is to save and invest over a long period of time. As a student, you might think that saving and investing is something you don't need to consider right now. But there's a cost to waiting, and even saving a little now can add up over time and help you pay for your short and long-term goals.

Keys to Financial Success

1. Make a financial plan.
2. Create a budget.
3. Start saving and investing as soon as you've paid off your debts.

YOUR FIRST STEP—MAKING A FINANCIAL PLAN

What Are the Things You Want to Save and Invest for?

- a car
- an education

- a comfortable social life
- emergencies
- periods of unemployment
- your future goals

Make your own list and then think about which goals are the most important to you. List your most important goals first.

Decide how many years you have to meet each specific goal, because when you save or invest you'll need to find a savings or investment option that fits your time frame for meeting each goal. Many tools exist to help you put your financial plan together.

YOUR FINANCIAL GOALS

If you don't know where you are going, you may end up somewhere you don't want to be. To end up where you want to be, you'll need a roadmap, a financial plan.

What do you want to save or invest for?	By when?
1. ______________________________	_______
2. ______________________________	_______
3. ______________________________	_______
4. ______________________________	_______
5. ______________________________	_______

You'll find a wealth of information, including calculators and links to non-commercial resources at **www.investor.gov**.

Know Your Current Financial Situation

Sit down and take an honest look at your entire financial situation. You can never take a journey without knowing where you're starting from, and a journey to financial comfort is no different. You'll need to figure out on paper your current situation—what you own and what you owe. You'll be creating a "net worth statement." On one side of the page, list what you own. These are your "assets." And on the other side list what you owe other people, your "liabilities" or debts.

YOUR NET WORTH STATEMENT			
Assets	**Current Value**	**Liabilities**	**Amount**
Cash	________	Credit cards	________
Checking accounts	________	Bank loans	________
Savings	________	Car loans	________
Other investments	________	Student loans	________
Personal property	________	Other	________
TOTAL	________	**TOTAL**	________

Subtract your liabilities from your assets. If your assets are larger than your liabilities, you have a "positive" net worth. If your liabilities are greater than your assets, you have a "negative" net worth.

You'll want to update your "net worth statement" every year to keep track of how you are doing. Don't be discouraged if you have a negative net worth. If you follow a plan to get into a positive position, you're doing the right thing.

Know Your Income and Expenses

The next step is to keep track of your income and your expenses for every month. Write down what you earn, and then your monthly expenses.

Pay Yourself First

Include a category for savings and investing. What are you paying yourself every month? Many people get into the habit of saving and investing by following this advice: always pay yourself first. Many people find it easier to pay themselves first if they allow their bank to automatically remove money from their paycheck and deposit it into a savings or investment account. If you work, you may be eligible to participate in an employer-sponsored retirement plan such as a 401(k), 403(b), or 457(b). That automatically deducts money from your paycheck, and may reduce the taxes you are paying. Additionally, in many plans the employer matches some or all of your contribution. When your employer does that, it's offering "free money." Any time you have automatic deductions made from your paycheck or bank account, you'll increase the chances of being able to stick to your plan and to realize your goals.

Finding Money to Save or Invest

If you are spending all your income, and never have money to save or invest, you'll need to look for ways to cut back on your expenses. When you watch where you spend your money, you will be surprised how small everyday expenses that you can do without add up over a year.

KNOW YOUR INCOME AND WHAT YOU SPEND	
Monthly Income	________
Monthly Expenses	________
Savings	________
Investments	________
Rent or mortgage	________
Telephone	________
Utilities	________
Clothing	________
Food	________
Transportation	________
Loans	________
Insurance	________
Education	________
Music	________
Recreation	________
Gifts	________
Other	________
TOTAL	________

SMALL SAVINGS ADD UP TO BIG MONEY

How Much Does a Bottle of Soda Cost You?

If you buy a bottle of soda every day for $2.00, that adds up to $730.00 a year. If you saved that $730.00 for just one year, and put it into a savings account or investment that earns 5% a year, it would grow to $931.69 after 5 years, and grow to $3,155.02 after 30 years.

That's the power of "compounding." With compound interest, you ear n interest on the money you save and on the interest that money ear ns. Over time, even a small amount saved can add up to big money.

If you are willing to watch what you spend and look for little ways to save on a regular schedule, you can make money grow. You just did it with one bottle of soda.

If a bottle of soda can make such a huge difference, start looking at how you could make your money grow if you decided to spend less on other things and save those extra dollars.

If you buy on impulse, make a rule that you'll always wait 24 hours to buy anything. You may lose your desire to buy it after a day. And try emptying your pockets and wallet of spare change at the end of each day and put that money aside. You'll be surprised how quickly those nickels and dimes add up!

Pay off Credit Card or Other High Interest Debt

Speaking of things adding up, few investment strategies pay off as well as, or with less risk than, merely paying off all high interest debt you may have.

Many people have credit cards, some of which they've "maxed out" (meaning they've spent up to their credit limit). Credit cards can make it seem easy to buy expensive things when you don't have the cash in your pocket—or in the bank. But credit cards aren't free money.

Most credit cards charge high interest rates—as much as 18 percent or more—if you don't pay off your balance in full each month. If you owe money on your credit cards, the wisest thing you can do is pay off the balance in full as quickly as possible. Virtually no investment will give you the high returns you'll need to keep pace with an 18 percent interest charge. That's why you're better off eliminating all credit card debt before investing savings.

Once you've paid off your credit cards, you can budget your money and begin to save and invest. Here are some tips for avoiding credit card debt:

Put Away the Plastic

Don't use a credit card unless your debt is at a manageable level and you know you'll have the money to pay the bill when it arrives.

Know What You Owe

It's easy to forget how much you've charged on your credit card. Every time you use a credit card, write down how much you have spent and figure out how much you'll have to pay that month. Keep track of your accounts online. If you know you won't be able to pay your balance in full, try to figure out how much you can pay each month and how long it'll take to pay the balance in full.

Pay off the Card with the Highest Rate

If you've got unpaid balances on several credit cards, you should first pay down the card that charges the highest rate. Pay as much as you can toward that debt each month until your balance is once again zero, while still paying the minimum on your other cards.

Now, once you have paid off those credit cards and begun to set aside some money to save and invest, what are your choices?

MAKING MONEY GROW

The Two Ways to Make Money

There are basically two ways to make money.

1. You work for money.
Someone pays you to work for them or you have your own business.

2. Your money works for you.
You take your money and you save or invest it.

Your Money Can Work for You in Two Ways

Your money earns money. When your money goes to work, it may earn a steady paycheck. Someone pays you to use your money for a period of time. When you get your money back, you get it back plus "interest." Or, if you buy stock in a company that pays "dividends" to shareholders, the company may pay you a portion of its earnings on a regular basis. Your money can make an "income," just like you. You can make more money when you and your money work.

You buy something with your money that could increase in value. You become an owner of something that you hope increases in value over time. When you need your money back, you sell it, hoping someone else will pay you more for it. For instance, you collect comic books thinking they will increase in value over time. You expect to sell them in five, ten, or even twenty years when someone will buy them from you for a lot more money than you paid.

And sometimes, your money can do both at the same time—ear n a steady paycheck and increase in value.

The Differences between Saving and Investing

Saving

Your "savings" are usually put into the safest places, or products, that allow you access to your money at any time. Savings products include savings accounts, checking accounts, and certificates of deposit. Some deposits in these products may be insured by the Federal Deposit Insurance Corporation or the National Credit Union Administration. But there's a tradeoff for security and ready availability. Your money is paid a low wage as it works for you.

After paying off credit cards or other high interest debt, most smart investors put enough money in a savings product to cover an emergency, like sudden unemployment. Some make sure they have up to six months of their income in savings so that they know it will absolutely be there for them when they need it.

But how "safe" is a savings account if you leave all of your money there for a long time, and the interest it ear ns doesn't keep up with inflation? What if you save a dollar when it can buy a loaf of bread. But years later when you withdraw that dollar plus the interest you earned on it, it can only buy half a loaf? This is why many people put some of their money in savings, but look to investing so they can ear n more over long periods of time, say three years or longer.

Investing

When you "invest," you have a greater chance of losing your money than when you "save." The money you invest in securities, mutual funds, and other similar investments typically is not federally insured. You could lose your "principal"—the amount you've invested. But you also have the opportunity to ear n more money.

THE BASIC TYPES OF PRODUCTS	
Savings	**Investments**
Savings accounts	Bonds
Certificates of deposit	Stocks
Checking accounts	Mutual funds, Exchange-traded funds
	Real estate
	Commodities (gold, silver, etc.)

What About Risk?

All investments involve taking on risk. It's important that you go into any investment in stocks, bonds or mutual funds with a full understanding that you could lose some or all of your money in any one investment. While over the long term the stock market has historically provided around 10% annual returns (closer to 6% or 7% "real" returns when you subtract for the effects of inflation), the long term does sometimes take a rather long, long time to play out. Those who invested all of their money in the stock market at its peak in 1929 (before the stock market crash) would wait over 20 years to see the stock market return to the same level.

However, those that kept adding money to the market throughout that time would have done very well for themselves, as the lower cost of stocks in the 1930s made for some hefty gains for those who bought and held over the course of the next twenty years or more.

It is often said that the greater the risk, the greater the potential reward in investing, but taking on unnecessary risk is often avoidable. Investors best protect themselves against risk by spreading their money among various investments, hoping that if one investment loses money, the other investments will more than make up for those losses. This strategy, called "diversification," can be neatly summed up as, "Don't put all your eggs in one basket." Investors also protect themselves from the risk of investing all their money at the wrong time (think 1929) by following a consistent patter n of adding new money to their investments over long periods of time.

Once you've saved money for investing, consider carefully all your options and think about what diversification strategy makes sense for you. While the SEC cannot recommend any particular investment product, you should know that a vast array of investment products exists—including stocks and stock mutual funds, corporate and municipal bonds, bond mutual funds, certificates of deposit, money market funds, and U.S. Treasury securities.

Diversification can't ***guarantee*** that your investments won't suffer if the market drops. But it can improve the chances that you won't lose money, or that if you do, it won't be as much as if you weren't diversified.

What Are the Best Investments for Me?

The answer depends on when you will need the money, your goals, and if you will be able to sleep at night if you purchase a risky investment where you could lose your principal.

For instance, if you are saving for a long term goal, such as a college fund for a child, you may want to consider riskier investment products, knowing that if you stick to only the "savings" products or to less risky investment products, your money will grow too slowly—or, given inflation and taxes, you may ***lose*** the purchasing power of your money. A frequent mistake people make is putting money they will not need for a very long time in investments that pay a low amount of interest.

On the other hand, if you are saving for a short-term goal, five years or less, such as a car, you don't want to choose risky investments, because when it's time to sell, you may have to take a loss. Since investments often move up and down in value rapidly, you want to make sure that you can wait and sell at the best possible time.

What Are Investments All About?

When you make an investment, you are giving your money to a company or enterprise, hoping that it will be successful and pay you back with even more money.

Stocks and Bonds

Many companies offer investors the opportunity to buy either stocks or bonds. The example below shows you how stocks and bonds differ.

Let's say you believe that a company that makes computers may be a good investment. Everyone you know is buying one of their computers, and your friends report that the company's laptops rarely break down and run well for years. You either have an investment professional investigate the company and read as much as possible about it, or you do it yourself.

After your research, you're convinced it's a solid company that will sell many more computers in the years ahead. The computer company offers both stocks and bonds. With the bonds, the company agrees to pay you back your initial investment in ten years, plus pay you interest twice a year at the rate of 4% a year. If you buy the stock, you take on the risk of potentially losing a portion or all of your initial investment if the company does poorly or the stock market drops in value. But you also may see the stock increase in value beyond what you could earn from the bonds. If you buy the stock, you become an "owner" of the company.

You wrestle with the decision. If you buy the bonds, you will get your money back plus the 4% interest a year. And you think the company will be able to honor its promise to you on the bonds because it has been in business for many years and doesn't look like it could go bankrupt. The company has a long history of making computers and you know that its stock has gone up in pr ice by an average of 6% a year, plus it has typically paid stockholders a dividend of 3% from its profits each year.

THE MAIN DIFFERENCES BETWEEN STOCKS AND BONDS	
Stocks	**Bonds**
If the company profits or is perceived as having strong potential, its stock may go up in value and pay dividends. You may make more money than from the bonds.	The company promises to return money plus interest.
Risk: The company may do poorly, and you'll lose a portion or all of your investment.	**Risk:** If the company goes bankrupt, your money may be lost. But if there is any money left, you will be paid before stockholders.

You take your time and make a careful decision. Only time will tell if you made the right choice. You'll keep a close eye on the company and keep the investment as long as the company keeps selling a quality computer that consumers want to use, and it can make an acceptable profit from its sales.

Why Some Investments Make Money and Others Don't

You can potentially make money in an investment in a company if:

- The company performs better than its competitors.
- Other investors recognize it's a good company, so that when it comes time to sell your investment, others want to buy it.

- The company makes profits, meaning they make enough money to pay you interest for your bond, or maybe dividends on your stock.

You can lose money if:

- Consumers don't want to buy the company's products or services.
- The company's officers mismanage the business, they spend too much money, and their expenses are larger than their profits.
- Other investors that you would need to sell to think the company's stock is too expensive given its performance and future outlook.
- The people running the company are ensnared in fraud.
- For whatever reason, you have to sell your investment when the market is down.

Mutual Funds

Because it is sometimes hard for investors to become experts on various businesses—for example, what are the best telecommunications, pharmaceutical, or computer companies—investors often depend on professionals who are trained to investigate companies and recommend companies that are likely to succeed. Since it takes work to pick the stocks or bonds of the companies that have the best chance to do well in the future, many investors choose to invest in mutual funds.

What Is a Mutual Fund?

A mutual fund is a pool of money run by a professional or group of professionals called the "investment adviser." In a managed mutual fund, after investigating the prospects of many companies, the fund's investment adviser will pick the stocks or bonds of companies and put them into a fund.

Investors can buy shares of the fund, and their shares rise or fall in value as the values of the stocks and bonds in the fund rise and fall. Investors may typically pay a fee when they buy or sell their shares in the fund, and those fees in part pay the salaries and expenses of the professionals who manage the fund.

Even small fees can and do add up and eat into a significant chunk of the returns a mutual fund is likely to produce, so you need to look carefully at how much a fund costs and think about how much it will cost you over the amount of time you plan to own its shares. If two funds are similar in every way except that one charges a higher fee than the other, you'll make more money by choosing the fund with the lower annual costs.

For more information about mutual fund fees and expenses, be sure to read our brochure entitled "Invest Wisely: An Introduction to Mutual Funds"—which you can read online at **www. sec.gov/investor/pubs/ inwsmf.htm** or order for free by calling **(888) 878-3256**.

Mutual Funds without Active Management

One way that investors can obtain for themselves nearly the full returns of the market is to invest in an "index fund." This is a mutual fund that does not attempt to pick and choose stocks of individual companies based upon the research of the mutual fund managers. An index fund seeks to equal the returns of a major stock market index, such as the Standard & Poor's 500, the Wilshire 5000, or the Russell 3000. Through computer programmed buying and selling, an index fund tracks the holdings of a chosen index, and so shows the same returns as an index minus, of course, the annual fees involved in running the fund. The fees for index mutual funds generally are much lower than the fees for managed mutual funds.

Historical data shows that index funds have, primarily because of their lower fees, enjoyed higher returns than the average managed mutual fund. But, like any investment, index funds involve risk.

Watch "Turnover" to Avoid Paying Excess Taxes

To maximize your mutual fund returns, or any investment returns, know the effect that taxes can have on what actually ends up in your pocket. Mutual funds that trade quickly in and out of stocks will have what is known as "high turnover." While selling a stock that has moved up in pr ice does lock in a profit for the fund, this is a profit for which taxes have to be paid. Turnover in a fund creates taxable capital gains, which are paid by the mutual fund shareholders. All mutual funds are now mandated by the SEC to show both their before- and after- tax returns. The differences between what a fund is reportedly earning, and what a fund is earning after taxes are paid on the dividends and capital gains, can be quite striking. If you plan to hold mutual funds in a taxable account, be sure to check out these historical returns in the mutual fund prospectus to see what kind of taxes you might be likely to incur.

HOW CAN I PROTECT MYSELF?

Ask Questions!

Many people hire an investment professional to assist in selecting investments. You can never ask a dumb question about your investments and the people who help you choose them, especially when it comes to how much you will be paying for any investment, both in upfront costs and ongoing management fees.

Here are some questions you should ask when choosing an investment professional or someone to help you:

- What training and experience do you have? How long have you been in business?
- What is your investment philosophy? Do you take a lot of risks or are you more concerned about the safety of my money?
- Describe your typical client. Can you provide me with references, the names of people who have invested with you for a long time?
- How do you get paid? By commission? Based on a percentage of assets you manage? Another method? Do you get paid more for selling your own firm's products?
- How much will it cost me in total to do business with you?

Your investment professional should understand your investment goals, whether you're saving to buy a car, or to pay for your education.

Your investment professional should ***also*** understand your tolerance for risk. That is, how much money can you afford to lose if the value of one of your investments declines? An investment professional has a duty to make sure that he or she only recommends investments that are suitable for you. That is, that the investment makes sense for you based on your other securities holdings, your financial situation, your means, and any other information that your investment professional thinks is important. The best investment professional is one who fully understands your objectives and matches investment recommendations to your goals. You'll want someone you can understand, because your investment professional should teach you about investing and the investment products.

How Should I Monitor My Investments?

Investing makes it possible for your money to work for you. In a sense, your money has become your employee, and that makes you the boss. You'll want to keep a close watch on how your employee, your money, is doing.

Some people like to look at the stock quotations every day to see how their investments have done. That's probably too often. You may get too caught up in the ups and downs of the "trading" value of your investment, and sell when its value goes down temporarily—even though the performance of the company is still stellar. Remember, you're in for the long haul.

Some people prefer to see how they're doing once a year. That's probably not often enough. What's best for you will most likely be somewhere in between, based on your goals and your investments.

But it's not enough to simply check an investment's performance. You should compare that performance against an index of similar investments over the same period of time to see if you are getting the proper returns for the amount of risk that you are assuming. You should also compare the fees and commissions that you're paying to what other investment professionals charge.

While you should monitor performance regularly, you should pay close attention ***every*** time you send your money somewhere else to work.

Every time you buy or sell an investment you will receive a confirmation slip from your broker. Make sure each trade was completed according to your instructions. Make sure the buying or selling pr ice was what your broker quoted. And make sure the commissions or fees are what your broker said they would be.

Watch out for unauthorized trades in your account. If you get a confirmation slip for a transaction that you didn't approve beforehand, call your broker. It may have been a mistake. If your broker refuses to correct it, put your complaint in writing and send it to the firm's compliance officer. Serious complaints should always be made in writing.

Remember, too, that if you rely on your investment professional for advice, he or she has an obligation to recommend investments that match your investment goals and tolerance for risk. Your investment professional should not be recommending trades simply to generate commissions. That's called "churning," and it's illegal.

How Can I Avoid Problems?

Choosing someone to help you with your investments is one of the most important investment decisions you will ever make. While most investment professionals are honest and hardworking, you must watch out for those few unscrupulous individuals. They can make your life's savings disappear in an instant.

Securities regulators and law enforcement officials can and do catch these criminals. But putting them in jail doesn't always get your money back. Too often, the money is gone. The good news is you can avoid potential problems by protecting yourself.

Make sure the investment professional and her firm are registered with the SEC and licensed to do business in your state. And find out from your state's securities regulator whether the investment professional or her firm have ever been disciplined, or whether they have any complaints against them.

IMPORTANT CONTACTS	
SEC	**NASAA**
100 F Street, N.E. Washington, D.C. 20549-0213 Toll-free: (800) 732-0330 Website: www.investor.gov	750 First Street, N.E., Suite 1140 Washington, D.C. 20002 Phone: (202) 737-0900 Website: www.nasaa.org

You'll find contact information for securities regulators in the U.S. by visiting the website of the North American Securities Administrators Association (NASAA) at www.nasaa.org or by calling (202) 737-0900.

You should also find out as much as you can about any investments that your investment professional recommends.

First, make sure the investments are registered. Keep in mind, however, the mere fact that a company has registered and files reports with the SEC doesn't guarantee that the company will be a good investment.

Be wary of promises of quick profits, offers to share "inside information," and pressure to invest before you have an opportunity to investigate. These are all warning signs of fraud. Ask your investment professional for written materials and prospectuses, and read them before you invest. If you have questions, now is the time to ask.

- How will the investment make money?
- How is this investment consistent with my investment goals?

- What must happen for the investment to increase in value?
- What are the risks?
- Where can I get more information?

Finally, it's always a good idea to write down everything your investment professional tells you. Accurate notes will come in handy if ever there's a problem.

Some investments make money. Others lose money. That's natural, and that's why you need a diversified portfolio to minimize your risk. But if you lose money because you've been cheated, that's not natural, that's a problem.

Call or write to us and let us know about the problem. Investor complaints are very important to the SEC. You may think you're the only one experiencing a problem, but typically, you're not alone. Sometimes it takes only one investor's complaint to trigger an investigation that exposes an illegal scheme. Complaints can be filed online with us by going to **www.sec.gov/complaint.shtml**.

KEEP IN TOUCH WITH US

We hope that you've found this brochure helpful. Please let us know how it can be improved.

We've only covered the basics, and there's a lot more to learn about saving and investing. But you'll be learning as you go and over your lifetime.

As we said at the beginning, the most important thing is to get started. And remember to ask questions as you make your investment decisions.

Be sure to find out if the person is licensed to sell investments, and if the investment is registered with us. So, we look forward to hearing from you. And in the years ahead, let us know how well your money is growing.

SEC
OFFICE *of* INVESTOR EDUCATION *and* ADVOCACY

U.S. Securities and Exchange Commission
Office of Investor Education and Advocacy

100 F Street, N.E.
Washington, D.C. 20549-0213
Toll-free: (800) 732-0330
Website: www.investor.gov

To order this publication for your classroom, please visit www.pueblo.gsa.gov. To order by phone, call the Federal Citizen Information Center at (888)878-3256 Monday-Friday 8am to 8pm ET.

SAVING AND INVESTING FOR STUDENTS GLOSSARY

Annual Return—An annual rate of return is the profit or loss on an investment over a one-year period. There are many ways of calculating the annual rate of return. If the rate of return is calculated on a monthly basis, the monthly rate can be multiplied by 12 to express an annual rate of return. This is often called the annual percentage rate (A.P.R.).

Asset—Any tangible or intangible item owned by an individual or a firm that has value in an exchange. A bank account, a home, or shares of stock are all examples of assets.

Bonds—A bond is a debt security, similar to an IOU. When you purchase a bond, you are lending money to a government, municipality, corporation, federal agency, or other entity known as the issuer. In return for the loan, the issuer promises to pay you a specified rate of interest during the life of the bond and to repay the face value of the bond (the principal) when it "matures," or comes due. In contrast to bondholders who have IOUs from the issuer, shareholders are owners of the company they purchase.

Broker—An individual who acts as an intermediary between a buyer and seller, usually charging a commission to execute trades. Brokers are required to seek the best execution of trades they make for clients, and if they recommend investments to clients, those investments must be suitable for the client.

Capital Gain—This is the profit that comes when an investment is sold for more than the price the investor paid to buy it.

Cash—Money that can be used to pay for goods or services. Cash equivalents or "near cash" items are very safe holdings that can be easily converted to cash.

Certificate of Deposit—Interest-bearing accounts offered by banks and savings and loans, which are federally insured. CDs are like savings accounts but pay higher interest rates in exchange for tying up money for a set amount of time, which can be a period of months or up to five years. If the money is removed before the CD matures, the account holder will be subject to a financial penalty.

Commission—The fee paid to a broker to execute a trade, sometimes based on the size of the order and/or its dollar value. Discount and online brokerage firms may charge the same flat fee to execute trades, regardless of how large or small the order is.

Compound Interest—Interest paid on principal and on accumulated interest.

Diversification—Dividing investments among different kinds of assets, such as stocks and bonds, with different risks and rewards, so as to minimize the potential harm from any one asset.

Dividends—A portion of a company's profit paid to shareholders. Public companies that pay dividends usually do soon a fixed schedule although they can issue them at any time. Unscheduled dividend payments are known as special dividends.

Exchange Traded Fund—A security that tracks price changes for an index, such as the Standard & Poor's 500 Index, or a commodity or a basket of assets, and which trades like a stock on an exchange.

Financial Planner—An investment professional who typically prepares financial plans for his or her clients. The kinds of services financial planners offer can vary widely. Some financial planners assess every aspect of a client's financial life—including saving, investments, insurance, taxes, retirement, and estate planning—and helps the client develop a detailed strategy or financial plan. Other professionals call themselves financial planners, but they may only be able to recommend investments in a narrow range of products that may or may not include securities.

Financial Security—Having an appropriate financial plan and enough financial resources to adequately fulfill any needs or most wants of an individual or business.

Inflation—A general upward movement in the price of goods or services is known as inflation. Supply and demand and the amount of money in circulation can increase inflation. Over time, inflation erodes the purchasing power of a currency, making the currency worth less. It also erodes the value of fixed payments to bondholders, one of the risks of investing in fixed-income securities.

Interest—The price paid for borrowing money. It is expressed as a percentage rate over a period of time. Interest rates may be fixed, meaning the rate is set and will not change, or may be variable or "floating," meaning the rate may move higher or lower over time.

Invest—To engage in any activity in which money is put at risk in the hope of making a profit.

Investment Adviser—An investment professional who gives advice to clients about investing in stocks, bonds, mutual funds or other assets. Some investment advisers also manage portfolios of securities. By law, investment advisers are required to act in the best interest of their customers.

Liability/Debt—An amount owed to a person or organization for borrowed funds. Loans, notes, bonds and mortgages are forms of debt. These different forms all call for borrowers to pay back the amount they owe, typically with interest, by a specific date, which is set forth in the repayment terms.

Money Market Funds—An investment fund that seeks to earn interest for shareholders while maintaining a stable net asset value (NAV) of $1 per share. Mutual funds, brokerage firms and banks offer these funds, which are not federally insured.

Mutual Funds—These are pools of money managed by an investment company. They offer investors a way to hold stocks, bonds or other assets. Funds are managed to meet certain objectives. Some funds may seek to generate income on a regular basis, for instance, while others may seek to invest in companies that are growing at a rapid pace. Funds usually charge annual management fees and may impose a sales charge, or load, on investors when they buy or sell shares in the fund. So-called "no load" funds impose no sales charge.

Principal—The total amount of money being borrowed or lent; the initial amount of money invested.

Profit—Revenue minus cost; money made on a transaction.

Purchasing Power—The amount of goods and services that can be purchased by a given unit of currency after taking into account the effect of inflation.

Real Return—The return that is earned over a given time period after subtracting taxes and accounting for inflation.

Risk—In finance, risk refers to the degree of uncertainty about the rate of return on an asset and the potential harm that could arise when financial returns are not what the investor expected. In general, as investment risks go up, investors seek higher returns to compensate them for taking on such risks.

Risk Tolerance—An investor's ability to handle declines or swings in the value of his or her portfolio.

Savings—Income that is not spent on consumption but is put aside.

Security—A stock, bond, or another investment.

Stocks—An instrument that represents partial ownership (called equity) of a corporation, and a claim on a proportional share of the corporation's assets and profits. Ownership in the company is determined by the number of shares a person owns divided by the total number of shares outstanding. Most stock also provides voting rights, which give shareholders a proportional vote in certain corporate decisions, such as the election of corporate directors.

Stock Market—A general term for the organized trading of stocks through exchanges, over-the-counter and computerized trading venues.

Stock Quotes—Listings of pr ices to buy and sell a specific stock. During trading, quotes show bids, the pr ices buyers are willing to pay, and offers, the pr ices sellers are willing to accept, in real time. Historical data for past trading provides the opening and closing price, and the daily high and low pr ice for a stock, along with trading volume.

Index

D

E

F

P

Q

R

S

T

U

V

W

Y